Published in Scottsdale, Arizona
30600 N. Pima Rd. #106
Scottsdale, AZ 85266

Edited by Roberta Landman

Design by Ashli Truchon

Digital Imaging by Frank Fernandez

Printed in the U.S.A.

Library of Congress Control Number: 2015931044

ISBN: 978-0-9855190-1-8

First Edition

On the cover: Michael William Phalen, a Union Army adjutant in the Civil War, had this photo taken in 1864 by J.J. Hawes, Photographers, in Boston after he was mustered out of the service. Photo of Grennan Castle, near Thomastown, Ireland, courtesy of National Monuments Service, Dept. of Arts, Heritage and the Gaeltacht, Dublin.

A Collection of Irish Grandfathers

Tracing the Phalens From 18th-Century
Ireland to North America—a Tribute From
William "Bill" Phalen to His Ancestors

WILLIAM "BILL" PHALEN
WITH ROBERTA LANDMAN

This genealogic study of my family's exodus from 19th-century Ireland and eventual resettlement in America is dedicated to my cousin Geraldine "Gerie" Abbatiello, who, with her husband, Aurie, lovingly and vigorously dug through any number of historic records and city directories to help me trace the Phalens' roots.

—WILLIAM "BILL" PHALEN

CONTENTS

Using a vintage photo as a guide, fine artist Russell Recchion painted this portrait of Michael William Phalen, William "Bill" Phalen's great-grandfather, who served in the Union Army during the U.S. Civil War.

ACKNOWLEDGMENTS

Learning the history of my family from the 18th to 20th centuries in Ireland, Nova Scotia, Canada, and eventually the United States was like fitting together pieces of a jigsaw puzzle with some pieces forever missing. Solve it I did, but not alone. I had help from some family members, and encouragement from friend Tom Crowley, who had traced his own family's roots. Russ Recchion, a Tucson, Arizona, artist, discovered valuable information about my great-grandfather, Michael William Phalen, who had served in the U.S. Civil War, and Russ ended up painting a fine portrait of him.

I also had assistance from professional genealogists Virginia Clark of Nova Scotia, Canada, and Rhonda R. McClure, Senior Researcher, New England Historic Genealogical Society.

Helpful information about my Irish immigrant family in Nova Scotia was found in books by Canadian genealogical expert and author Terrence M. Punch. He chronicled the history of the Irish in Atlantic Canada from 1761-1853.

Finally, the U.S. Civil War, and my Irish-American family's role in it, became more than dry history-book facts when seen through the lens of writer/historian Christian G. Samito. He brought the Civil War and Irish-American involvement in it to life in a personal way for me in several of his endeavors.

MY THANKS TO ALL.
—WILLIAM "BILL" PHALEN

preface

FINDING MICHAEL WILLIAM PHALEN

All of us are interested in where we came from. This curiosity develops slowly and usually doesn't mature until later in life.

About a dozen or so years ago I accumulated enough information to begin a search of my ancestors from their time in Ireland to their sailing to Halifax, Nova Scotia, Canada, in the early 1800s.

The family patriarch was Maurice Phelan, born in 1772; married to Eleanor Murphy in 1796, in Thomastown parish, County Kilkenny, Ireland; and said to have lived in the townland of Dangan. They had seven children: three girls and four boys, between 1796 and 1817.

Eleanor Murphy Phelan likely died between 1817 and 1820. Shortly after, Maurice married Mary Murphy and they had one child. Was Mary Eleanor's sister? We don't know.

It is believed that neither wife nor Maurice and Eleanor's son Patrick and their daughters Mary, Elizabeth, and Judith—and Ellen, his daughter with Mary Murphy Phelan—ever left Ireland.

Maurice and his three sons possibly left Ireland and sailed to Halifax, Nova Scotia, between 1825 and 1832. In 1825, Maurice would have been fifty-three years of age, son Edward, twenty-nine, Lawrence approximately sixteen, and Michael, eight. Maurice and his sons would never see Ireland again, nor the relatives and friends left behind. Once they settled in Halifax, they had to squeeze out a meager living in a very small economy. Survive they did.

About the time my research seemed to be hitting a dead end, a friend suddenly discovered a Civil War bio of Michael William Phalen in a Pennsylvania antique shop. After matching this discovery with my research files, I was able to confirm that Michael was my great-grandfather.

IV

Finding Michael's spirit was the best discovery: One, he invigorated the whole research project and two, Michael authenticates his status as a Civil War hero and entrepreneur.

Michael William Phalen was born in 1842, the son of Lawrence, and grandson of Maurice. Shortly after the death of his father in 1847, Michael moved to Salem, Massachusetts, in 1848 with his mother, brother Edward, and three sisters. At the age of nineteen, Michael enlisted in the Ninth Regiment Massachusetts Volunteer Infantry in Boston, Massachusetts. He gave his age as twenty-one, for fear that on account of his youth he would risk acceptance.

Michael was injured in two Civil War engagements, once by a wound to the forehead from a piece of shell, and on another occasion he was struck on the hip by an unexploded ricocheting shell. These injuries suggest to me that Michael was fighting in very close quarters. He stayed on the battlefield on both occasions, and was recognized for bravery, having been with his regiment in every engagement.

For three years Michael battled on the front, sleeping outdoors in bivouac conditions and marching from battle to battle. His was a nasty business, being in a constant state of readiness.

Michael sped through the ranks from First Sergeant of Co. F to Second Lieutenant Sept. 7, 1861, as First Lieutenant Jan. 28, 1862, and appointed Adjutant of the regiment Aug. 28, 1862.

After the war, Michael moved back to Salem for a brief time to plan a leather goods business in Chicago. Michael moved to Chicago sometime in 1864. He was successful until the Great Chicago Fire, October 8-10, 1871, swept away his modest fortune and all of his possessions. He then relocated to Boston to establish a new leather goods business, but it, too, was destroyed by the Great Boston Fire, November 9-10, 1872. Not to be discouraged, Michael returned to Chicago to begin anew, and ultimately had a successful career in the steel business.

Michael was married three times: first to Ellen Fay of Boston, who died in 1863, not long after they were married; to his second wife, Margaret "Maggie" Ryan, who died in 1873; and to his third wife, Mary Curtin, who survived Michael for twenty years after his death in 1908.

Michael fathered nine children, but only three survived to grow into manhood. Michael had five children with Margaret and only one survived—my grandfather. Michael and Mary had four children, and only two sons lived to adulthood.

Michael lived in a world of great pain but plenty of opportunity. He took on many roles: emigrant, Adjutant of the Ninth, father, husband to three wives, traveling salesman and entrepreneur.

Within the pages of this family history, one will find a Civil War hero, a man with a great capacity to survive the loss of two businesses from fire and six children at very early ages. Yet, he had the strength and determination to prevail, just as he did living in the wilderness for three years risking his life daily—in one battle after another.

There is something special about Michael. He comes to life in the pages of this family history.

—*William "Bill" Phalen*

INTRODUCTION

illiam "Bill" Phalen's quest for knowledge of his ancestors has seen this 21st-century American traveling to Ireland, and also to cemeteries in New England, Illinois and Nova Scotia, to find the graves of long-gone relatives.

The thrill of the hunt—over more than a decade of information-gathering—has evolved into one of respect for those who came before him, such as Irish family patriarch Maurice Phelan, Bill's great-great-great grandfather, and U.S. Civil War veteran brothers Michael William Phalen and Edward Augustus Phalen; Michael was Bill's great-grandfather. The story of these two brothers puts a human, Every Man face on those who fought in this terrible conflict, which nearly tore a nation apart.

This foray into Bill Phalen's family history is presented in the context of what was happening during the time in which three generations lived: during poverty-wracked late-18th- and early-19th-century Ireland, during an immigration hiatus in Nova Scotia, and then in the United States, where the family finally set down roots. In a broader view, their story is a reminder of the coming of immigrants to America from the world over, the obstacles they have had to face and overcome, and their dreams of opportunity.

PROLOGUE

Civil War Union Army sword that Bill Phalen had seen in his childhood home sparked his curiosity about its tie to his family and to a vintage photo of a man in a military jacket.

In recent years, he began a genealogical trip into the past that has taken him back to his great-great-great-grandfather, Maurice Phelan, born in the 18th century in County Kilkenny, Ireland.

Doing much of his own investigating, he also engaged the services of the New England Historic Genealogical Society (NEHGS) and a Canadian genealogist. A genealogically savvy cousin and others who caught his fire along the way also helped. Excitement mounted as records requested from the National Archives and Records Administration (NARA) provided details about two ancestors' brave Civil War involvement; one of them was Bill's great-grandfather, the owner of that sword and the man in the old photo.

Figuring out who was who in the Phalen line saw the NEHGS researchers looking for answers in numerous places. Among them were the Church of Jesus Christ of Latter-day Saints Family History Library (FHL) in Salt Lake City, Utah, and such archaic-looking handwritten Irish baptism records of the Catholic Church's Thomastown parish, from the late-18th and early-19th centuries. Baptism dates often were found, for the important religious rite marked an infant's entrance into the Church, and, along with other sacraments, "entry to the kingdom of heaven."[1]

PHELANS AND PHALENS—THE SAME FOLK

Initially, searching for the name Phalen itself turned out to be more complicated than one would think. At times, records show that the people being sought in a genealogical pursuit have had different spellings of their names, or different names altogether: hence the spellings of Bill Ph*alen* and ancestor Maurice Ph*elan*. In fact, Maurice and his kin variously had their surnames spelled as Whelan after relocating to Nova Scotia, adding challenge to the search.

Several sources have attributed the shifting name changes to clerics, clerks and other scribes of Ireland in centuries past who wrote down anglicized versions of names as they heard them. In his book "Genealogical Research in Nova Scotia," Canadian genealogical historian Terrence M. Punch states that names found in a search can be "distorted" in many ways. "An ancestor may not have known the spelling of his or her name to begin with. The illiterate would not have been the wiser if their name were recorded incorrectly. Thus, names were often heard and recorded by 'ear.'"[2] Genealogist Angus Baxter suggests: "The changes usually occurred because few people could spell in older days, and there was no absolutely correct spelling. Therefore, at baptisms, marriages and burials, names were often written in the church registers as they sounded."[3]

As far as the *Phelan* surname is concerned, its various spellings are all English versions of the same Irish Gaelic name, say sources. That old Gaelic surname was O Faolain.[4]

The result: In early-19th-century Halifax, Nova Scotia, the church burial record for Maurice Phelan, who died May 28, 1837, shows his last name as Whelan.[5] And then, while Irish church baptism records for the sons who moved to Nova Scotia show them as Phelans, in Halifax's church marriage records they were registered as Whelans.[6]

When Bill Phalen's ancestors put down roots in the United States, initially in Massachusetts, Phalen, with an "a" in the first syllable and an "e" in the last, presumably became the surname spelling of choice. But that did not stop different spellings from creeping into a variety of records in the United States along the span of years.

Genealogical clues were discovered in a variety of records from the family's years in Nova Scotia and Massachusetts as well. Professional researchers, and Bill Phalen and his cousin, pored over such old sources as census reports, newspaper accounts, area directories, Civil War military records, and more. Some measure of this sleuthing has been by deduction, by comparing bits of known information. An example: It can be deduced that Maurice Phelan and sons left Ireland before the infamous Potato Famine of the mid-1840s to 1850s, when so many emigrated from Ireland, because

Nova Scotia records show that the sons were married there, beginning in 1832.[7]

This was but one solved mystery in the Phelan family "detective" story. Many more illuminations would follow, including learning the differences between Irish geographic/religious/civil terminology—a patchwork quilt of overlapping, intersecting jurisdictional boundaries called townlands, parishes and baronies that ultimately leads to knowledge of one's ancestors. A related story, *Looking for Irish Ancestors: A Short Course,* sheds some light on this nitty-gritty stuff.

WHAT'S IN A NAME?

As in many cultures, Irish babies often have been named after relatives their parents wish to honor, and the Phelan/Phalen family appears somewhat to have followed this tradition: The family tree is peppered with duplicate first, or given, names over multiple generations.

For example, there are several Lawrences (also recorded as Laurence), Edwards, Michaels (at least once noted as Michel) and Williams (like Bill Phalen himself; and his grandfather on his father's side also was William). The women, too, over years have had the same given name, or a derivative thereof. The name of patriarch Maurice Phelan's wife Eleanor, for instance, takes various forms: In records she also is referred to as Nelly or Ellen. Ellens, as well as Marys and Margarets, abound in the family story. There also is an Ann, and there is an Anna, and some records attribute various and similar spellings to each. (Confused? Don't give up yet.)

"Star players" in the Phelan/Phalen family saga do become clearer as their story progresses, leading up to Bill Phalen's best discovery and pride and joy—his great-grandfather, Michael William Phalen, a U.S. Civil War veteran.

chapter 1

FAREWELL: AN ILL WIND BLOWS

A ruin near Thomastown, County Kilkenny, Ireland, Grennan Castle was built in the 13th century by the area's Anglo-Norman ruling official, Thomas FitzAnthony. Today, livestock graze around it, as in this bucolic scene, and roam freely through it as well. Photo courtesy of National Monuments Service, Dept. of Arts, Heritage and the Gaeltacht, Dublin.

An Old Irish Blessing

May the road rise up to meet you,
May the wind ever be at your back,
May the sun shine warm upon your face,
And rains fall soft upon your fields,
And until we meet again,
May God hold you in the palm of His hand.

I

ow many generations of Irish people—leaving their homeland in search of a better life—must have been sent off with sentiments such as that old Irish blessing. Maurice Phelan of Thomastown, County Kilkenny, Ireland, and three of his four sons, Edward ("Edmund"), Lawrence and Michael, might have heard such words from loved ones and friends as they set sail during the first half of the 19th century for Halifax, Nova Scotia.

Why the Phelans left Ireland may be the result of a single cause or a combination of historic factors: Among them were lack of employment, poverty and the threat of starvation, or the effects on their country of a long history of British rule that ranged from thwarting their right to worship as Catholics, to not allowing them to give their children a Catholic education, to putting severe restrictions on their ownership of land.

The weather, too, seemed to conspire against the agrarian country and its people, at intervals ruining crops and causing several famines even before the notorious Irish Potato Famine of the 1840s that killed great numbers of people and caused multitudes to flee. The Ireland that Maurice and the others were born into was a land stricken with poverty; many were reduced to near-starvation diets when the small plots of land they leased and tilled failed to produce the food they desperately needed.

Periods of extremely low temperatures had disastrous effects on their meager crops, leading to hunger, malnutrition, disease and deaths, and also several famines, states historian Brian Fagan in "The Little Ice Age: How Climate Made History, 1300-1850." The Irish, he writes, who largely had subsisted on cereals, oats and, for centuries, potatoes, endured a "terrible famine in the exceptional cold of 1740 and 1741, when both the grain and potato crops failed."[1] Later, he writes, "A serious food shortage developed in 1782/83, when cold, wet weather destroyed much of the grain crop at the height of a major economic slump."[2] Maurice Phelan would have experienced such hardships as a child living in the 18th century. As he grew into manhood, he would witness and experience many disruptions in daily life—the pangs of a hungry belly, perhaps, as his town, like his country, underwent economic changes while being pelted with catastrophes of nature and doomed enterprise.

If others who left Ireland are examples, then the Phelans did not leave Ireland and family behind because things were going well for them.

chapter II

MAURICE'S THOMASTOWN

Grennan Mill, an 18th-century grain mill on the River Nore at Thomastown, Ireland, was still functioning into the 20th century. Recent times see it a venue for art education. Photo courtesy of National Monuments Service, Dept. of Arts, Heritage and the Gaeltacht, Dublin.

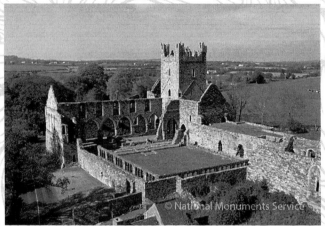

An atmospheric ruin, Jerpoint Abbey, near Thomastown, County Kilkenny, Ireland, dates back to the 12th century and a Cistercian order of monks. Photo courtesy of National Monuments Service, Dept. of Arts, Heritage and the Gaeltacht, Dublin.

Originally built in the 18th century, and repaired various times due to flood damage, this stone bridge still is being used in Thomastown, County Kilkenny, Ireland. Photo courtesy of Coilin O'Drisceoil, Kilkenny Archaeology, Kilkenny City, Ireland.

II

aurice Phelan was born about 1772[1] in County Kilkenny, Ireland, in the province of Leinster. While his parentage is unknown, he may have grown up in Thomastown, for he later would marry and raise a family there, in the townland of Dangan, barony of Gowran. He wed Eleanor (Nelly) Murphy October 16, 1796, in Thomastown parish,[2] and they had a big family, seven children—three girls and four boys—born between the years 1796 and 1817.[3] After Eleanor died, he remarried and had another daughter.

Putting two and two together from various sources, it is believed that neither wife nor Maurice and Eleanor's son Patrick and their daughters Mary, Elizabeth and Judith—and Ellen, his daughter with second wife Mary Murphy Phelan—ever left Ireland, and that Maurice's wives likely had died in Thomastown by 1825,[4] before he left the country. Those who did emigrate might have done so as early as 1825 and as late as 1832.[5]

The Thomastown that the Phelans knew had been around for centuries by the time they came on the scene. It was founded around the year 1200, during Ireland's Norman Conquest, by Thomas FitzAnthony, an Anglo-Norman seneschal [administrator or governor] of Leinster.[6] Thomastown, once a medieval fortified area, is said to have been named for him.

By 1731, forty-some years before Maurice was born, the population of Thomastown and vicinity was 1,144; by 1800, when Maurice was a father of two, the population was nearly 4,000. Thomastown (the town) that same year had about three hundred and fifty houses, fifty more than it had in 1792.[7]

From medieval times, Thomastown was a bustling place; it had served as an in-between point for transporting goods from ports of New Ross and Waterford south of Thomastown up to Kilkenny on the River Nore, twelve miles to the north.[8] Maurice the boy might have seen his father laboring on a dock, or engaged in some other sort of river commerce. Maurice himself might have worked in similar fashion at the river to support his own growing family.

Details of how he earned his living in Ireland are unknown and open to speculation. He might have been a fisherman, catching and selling the River Nore's then-plentiful salmon and trout. Perhaps he was a stonemason and called upon in 1792, when he was 20, to help rebuild the old stone Thomastown River Nore bridge; with an unlucky history, it also had been damaged by a flood in 1763.[9] Maybe his ancestors helped put it back together way back then. With some modifications over the years, the bridge still stands today. Was Maurice a man of the earth—one of the many Irish tenant farmers? Or, by some chance, did he have a bit of land of his own to cultivate? Not known.

While scholars say a preponderance of Irish of the time eked out an existence as laborers or as peasant farmers (cottiers) on British-owned Irish land, others looked to other ways to stave off impending poverty. Notes author David Dickson: "Most eighteenth-century Irish towns contained many families who worked at home as piece-workers or as independent artisans in textiles, the clothing and leather trades, or food processing."[10] Did Maurice and his kin work in the leather trades? Interestingly, many years later in America, his grandson Michael William Phalen—Bill Phalen's great-grandfather—would engage in the leather trade in his own tanning businesses.

Other business activity also was taking place in Thomastown in the latter part of the eighteenth century. During that time, the area had small-scale manufacturing, artisanal activity and retailing, states author Marilyn Silverman in her comprehensive book "An Irish Working Class: Explorations in Political Economy and Hegemony, 1800-1950." Pointing to details in Ireland's *Lucas Directory* from the year 1788, Silverman says of Thomastown: "Its trade was illustrated by its three boat owners, three corn merchants, two spirits merchants, and a general merchant. Its manufacturing and artisanal activities were represented by three flour mills, a grist mill, a tannery, three malting houses, a skinner's shop, and a soap-boiling enterprise. Its retail function was exemplified by five drapers, three grocers, two chandlers, two vintners, an apothecary, an earthenware dealer, a liquor dealer, and an innkeeper."[11]

Maurice's antecedents, or he as well, might have sought work at any of those enterprises, such as a flour mill, for example. With a ready source of River Nore water for power, flour mills had sprouted riverside in Thomastown over time. One of them, an eighteenth-century stone structure, today functions as the Grennan Mill Craft School, and painters and photographers who seek to capture the structure's image are wooed by its old-time charm .[12]

A period of economic expansion in Thomastown did not last. At some point, reports Silverman, "millers and tanners were heavily in debt and the malting houses and distilleries were to have only short lifespans."[13] By 1815, she notes, both laborers and artisans in Thomastown were being "exploited as workers and consumers."[14] Adding insult to injury, the following year the weather again would bring disaster to the Irish and others. After a cycle of very cold years, there were catastrophic harvest failures in 1816 in Europe, North Africa and elsewhere, writes Brian Fagan. "The large number of beggars in Italy, Switzerland and Ireland contributed to a high mortality in those countries, largely from typhus and the diseases of famine and hunger," he states.[15] This was the world Maurice Phelan lived in as a married man having to provide for his family. By 1816, he already was the father of six.

If somehow he was able to keep food on the table and disease from his door, Maurice nonetheless may have lost hope in his country's future and begun thinking of emigrating. He would have witnessed Thomastown's shrinking opportunities. According to Silverman, "By the mid-1820s, as a result of changing markets, the post-1815 depression, and the growth of other urban centers, only a tannery, several grist mills, and two modernized flour mills remained."[16] Further, by the late 1820s, Thomastown's importance in river-borne trade diminished when the river became silty and hindered navigation. This exacerbated local poverty, writes Silverman, for a "main source of the town's wealth since the thirteenth century had been its head of navigation on the River Nore."[17]

LIFE UNDER BRITAIN'S THUMB

Irish Catholics had long been the objects of British oppression when Maurice was a child and into his manhood. In the 17th century and into the 18th century, Irish Catholics were subjected to a series of so-called Penal Laws devised by British authorities. One of the most critical rules affected the inheritance of property. While many Irish toiled for subsistence as tenant farmers on land of absentee British landlords, those Catholics who owned land (as well as others who were not Protestant) could not hand it down intact to the eldest son at their demise, which was the custom. Rather, they had to divide the land among all the sons, creating smaller and smaller parcels of lesser worth and poor productivity.[18] Under another penal law, the Catholic educational system was outlawed, and those who wanted their children educated by priests had to do so in clandestine ways. Illegal teaching sessions arose and were held in secret at ruins and other outdoor locations, and at times indoors; they became known as "hedge schools," for lore has it that some such lessons took place in hiding spots behind hedgerows.[19] Toward the end of the eighteenth century, the penal laws were gradually being relaxed, but the conditions and antagonism they spawned lingered long afterward and could very well have added to what fueled Maurice's decision to emigrate.

WEIGHING ONE'S OPTIONS: NOT MANY

If history is a guide, then the extreme poverty that was overtaking Ireland likely was the major factor in why Maurice and his three sons chose to leave all that was familiar to them; others had been doing that for the same reason. In a Thomastown parish marriage record, Maurice and Eleanor are said to have lived in the townland of Dangan.[20] Dangan later became part of the Poor Law Union of Thomastown, one of several Irish districts, complete with workhouses, created to help the poor.[21] While the Thomastown Poor Law Union came about in 1850, when Maurice and sons were long gone from Ireland, they likely had seen the "handwriting on the wall," had no hope of conditions getting better, and had the vision to emigrate when they did; or, they had no other choice but to leave.

The Phelans were so-called pre-Famine emigrants, people who left Ireland before the notorious Potato Famine, which struck around 1845. And they were not alone. "During the thirty years from the end of the Napoleonic Wars [1815] to the beginning of the Great Famine, between 800,000 and 1,000,000 emigrants—about twice the total size for the preceding two hundred years—sailed to North America," states author Kerby A. Miller in "Emigrants and Exiles: Ireland and the Irish Exodus to North America."[22] The Irish were relocating to America, Newfoundland and the Maritime provinces of New Brunswick and Nova Scotia, for example.

The greatest wave of Irish emigration is generally associated with the country's disastrous blight-caused potato crop failure of the 1840s, which resulted in the Potato Famine, known also by such names as the Great Famine and the Great Hunger. Some background: By the early 1840s, almost half of the Irish population, mostly the rural poor, depended almost exclusively on the potato for their diet. However, the varieties of plants they cultivated could not survive the blight and were decimated, leading to the infamous famine.[23] According to one estimate, between the years 1846 and 1850, the population of Ireland dropped by two million, about 25 percent of the total population. Half of that population loss is associated with deaths due to starvation or famine-associated diseases. The other million souls emigrated.[24]

Leaving Ireland before the historic famine, Maurice perhaps had looked forward to employment outlets in Halifax, Nova Scotia—in fishing, lumber, construction or other avenues—and then made the difficult decision to seek better opportunities across the North Atlantic.

chapter III

CONSIDERATIONS BEFORE EMIGRATING

The River Nore and the mood-evoking old Grennan Mill seem an artist's study
in Thomastown, County Kilkenny, Ireland. Photo courtesy of Coilin O'Drisceoil,
Kilkenny Archaeology, Kilkenny City, Ireland.

III

If the family was leaving Ireland around 1827, for example, Maurice was already fifty-five years old. Son Edward would have been around thirty-one years old, Lawrence around eighteen, and Michael a young boy of ten. Perhaps the Phelans left around this time, for fares had come down.

According to the Public Record Office of Northern Ireland (PRONI): "In 1827 the British government repealed the Passenger Acts, which had greatly inflated the cost of fares. That year, over 20,000 Irish took advantage of the cheaper rates. New, less stringent regulations were introduced in 1828, and between that date and 1837 almost 400,000 Irish immigrated to North America." The agency notes that by 1831 the standard fare from Ireland to Canada (depending on the season, the route taken and the shipping line) had dropped from an average of between four and ten pounds sterling to one pound ten shillings.[1]

And, if the Phelans left Ireland by 1830, their voyage would certainly have been long, but shorter than in previous times. The "technological improvements in sailing ships had significantly reduced the duration of the average Atlantic crossing, from eight to ten weeks in the 18th century to only five to six weeks by about 1830," notes Kerby A. Miller.[2]

If the Phelans worried about the trip's possible dangers, they had a right to be worried. States the PRONI report: "Although the Canadian route was relatively inexpensive, it was considered very hazardous. The death rate could be extremely high, whether from shipwreck or ship's fever [including typhoid fever and cholera]." Nonetheless, the report continues, many who would have preferred to go to America instead chose the Canadian route "because it was all they could afford and they later traveled overland to the United States."[3]

The Starting Point—a River Runs Through It

The Phelans might have made Waterford, about twenty-five miles south of Thomastown, their point of embarkation for the transatlantic sea voyage. Surely, it would have made life easier if they had been able to start their journey by catching a boat on the banks of the River Nore right at their own Thomastown "doorstep," so to speak. But the longstanding impediments to navigation—including places too shallow for a boat—between this point in the river and Inistioge, about seven miles south, made that impossible.

A notation about Thomastown and the river's condition in *A Topographical Dictionary, 1837,* stated: "The present town, in 1831, contained 527 houses, most of which are neatly built. Over the river Nore is a handsome stone bridge of five arches, built in 1792, at each end of which is an ancient square tower, formerly connected with the fortifications by which the town was surrounded. A very considerable trade was formerly carried on, and the town was the commercial depot for the county of Kilkenny; flat-bottomed boats of an aggregate burden of 11,000 tons were constantly employed in conveying goods from this town, besides many others which did not belong to it; but the river is now choked up with deposits of sand."[4]

The river at Thomastown, today popular with canoeing and kayaking enthusiasts, never did return to its one-time commercially navigable state. Locals, and tourists who travel to Ireland, also can trek beside the river on the recreational Nore Valley Walk, a route that extends from the city of Kilkenny to the north, through Thomastown and south to Inistioge.[5]

Leaving Ireland in the 1800s, under far more serious circumstances than recreation, the Phelans likely would have traveled by road from Thomastown and boarded a vessel on the River Nore at Inistioge. After the Nore merged with the River Barrow, they would have gone ashore at Waterford and boarded the ship that carried them across the ocean.

chapter IV

HALIFAX, NOVA SCOTIA

Fort George, atop Citadel Hill in Halifax, Nova Scotia, looms above the city's Old Town Clock. Built in the mid-18th century, the fort is now part of Canada's parks system as the Halifax Citadel National Historic Site. Vintage photo by W.R. MacAskill, courtesy of Nova Scotia Archives.

A Halifax, Nova Scotia, landmark, the Old Town Clock has been renovated since this vintage photo was taken by noted photographer W.R. MacAskill. It was Prince Edward, Duke of Kent, the father of England's famed Queen Victoria, who planned the unique structure at the dawn of the 19th century. Photo courtesy of Nova Scotia Archives.

Refurbished in the 1960s, the Old Town Clock has its original clockworks.

IV

While contemporary records occasionally will yield information about some who sailed on certain ships, full lists of Irish passengers arriving in Nova Scotia between 1815 and 1845 did not survive, writes genealogical historian Terrence M. Punch in "Erin's Sons: Irish Arrivals in Atlantic Canada, 1761-1853."[1] So, instead of ship information, gleanings from church birth, baptism, marriage and death records certify the Phelans' presence in Halifax.

Founded by Britain in 1749 as the capital of Nova Scotia, and as a naval and military post, Halifax is located on a peninsula that thrusts out into the Atlantic Ocean. The large natural Halifax Harbour became a British naval base, and, nearby, the summit of a hill became the site of a citadel, or fortress; it was built initially to protect the area from the French, who, since the early 17th century, had been engaged in a variety of conflicts with the British over control of what France named Acadia and England dubbed Nova Scotia (New Scotland). The Seven Years War, 1756-1763, in which England and France were engaged, cemented Nova Scotia's British rule.[2]

Like tourists and residents of Halifax today, the Phelans would have laid eyes on that British fortress, perched on Citadel Hill. Fortifications atop this bluff were rebuilt several times to serve British Halifax's defensive needs, including protection against American colonists during the American Revolution, and again during the U.S. Civil War, when the British were thought to have Southern sympathies.[3] Named Fort George, after Britain's King George II, the Halifax Citadel is now part of Canada's parks system as the Halifax Citadel National Historic Site.[4] Also a landmark to the arriving 19th-century Phelans and to folk of today, a multiple-tiered "Old Town Clock" tower is situated in the shadow of Halifax Citadel. For the Phelans, it would be a reminder that while they might have more opportunity in Nova Scotia than in British-dominated Ireland, British influence likewise held sway in their new land. The clock tower was commissioned by Prince Edward, Duke of Kent, Commander-in-Chief of the British military in North America, to remind the military troops there of the need for punctuality. It was his parting gesture before returning to England in 1800.[5]

Among people the Phelans would have noticed in this new land were the indigenous Mi'kmaqs. The area's original inhabitants, the Mi'kmaq tribe had made the initial contact with European explorers in the 16th century.[6] Acadian folk also were there when the Phelans arrived. Some had made their way back to Nova Scotia after the British had expelled them (1755-1762) for abstaining from allegiance to Britain, and for suspected French sympathies.[7] The notorious expulsion had sent many to Louisiana and as far away as France. Henry Wadsworth Longfellow's epic poem "Evangeline"—published in 1847—is set against that deportation.[8] Black people, too, were in Halifax: At the close of the American Revolution, many who lived in colonial America had been loyal to the British and fled to Nova Scotia.[9]

Halifax in its very early years had attracted Irish Catholics in search of employment, in particular for construction projects. "Though they were not encouraged to come [by the British] because of their religion and ethnicity, by 1767 there may have been 467 Irish Catholics in the area, constituting perhaps as much as 16 percent of the population," notes a report in *The Encyclopedia of Canada's Peoples*. The article further states: "From 1815 to 1838, nearly 11,000 Irish, mostly Catholics, arrived in Halifax, creating an invigorated minority that, by 1837, constituted more than one-third (35 percent) of the town's population."[10] Maurice Phelan, one of those statistics, lived to see all of this happening.

The type of work the Phelan men engaged in is not known, but, if they worked in construction, they might have applied for work on the Citadel fortress; it was still being built when they were in Halifax, and was not completed until 1856.[11]

Research shows that the sons of Maurice Phelan—Edward "Edmund", Lawrence and Michael—married and had families in Halifax. Although Maurice died in 1837 in Halifax at about age sixty-five,[12] he apparently lived long enough to enjoy the births of at least some of his grandchildren.[13-15]

Out of the Frying Pan, Into Much the Same Fire

As Irish Catholics, the Phelans may have experienced bigotry in the British Nova Scotia colony, as they quite likely had in Ireland; and this could have affected their future in Halifax. Notes an article in the *Canadian Encyclopedia*: "Because the Catholics were socially and politically disadvantaged in Ireland, they arrived in Canada with few advantages other than a familiarity with the English language and British institutions. They lacked the means to establish themselves securely within the economy and had little impact on the business community." By contrast, the article states that the Protestant Irish "generally had more money and found it significantly easier to re-establish themselves as farmers. They became one of the most agrarian groups in 19th-century Canada. Because their religion made them more acceptable to the dominant society, they were able to move much more freely in Canadian society."[16] Whether because of prejudice or want of opportunity, some of patriarch Maurice Phelan's family chose to relocate.

chapter V

A FUTURE IN AMERICA

In recent years, William "Bill" Phalen photographed this house at 39 Boardman St. in Salem, Mass., where his ancestor Edward Augustus Phalen and family once lived. It was built in 1885 and was still being used as a multi-unit residence when the photo was taken.

V

In a movie or a play, Maurice Phelan's son Lawrence Phelan and Lawrence's wife, Ann Johnston Phelan, would have major supporting roles. Parents of three girls and three boys, it was their two sons—Edward Augustus Phalen and Michael William Phalen—who went on to fight in the U.S. Civil War. Unfortunately, Lawrence Phelan did not live to see his children grow up, having passed away December 30, 1847. It was a time of change in the midst of turmoil. Sometime in 1848, Ann Johnston Phelan summoned her courage and began yet another chapter of her life in a second new country, the United States—destination Massachusetts—where Lawrence's brother Michael and his wife and two children had moved.

When she was single, Ann had the pluck to travel some 2,000 miles over several weeks across the stormy Atlantic Ocean to an uncertain future. Now, a widow with children in tow, she would face the uncertainty of how to care for them, without her husband, in a strange new place.

In 1848, the children ranged from teenagers down to a three-year-old. Daughters Margaret, Marianne and Ellen, were fourteen, twelve and three years old, respectively; son Lawrence was ten, Edward Augustus, eight, and Michael William, six. For whatever reasons, no evidence was found that young Lawrence ever moved with his mother, sisters and brothers to the United States; and it is not known whether Ann might have made a single journey to Massachusetts with the rest of the children, or a few trips back to Halifax to bring them to their new home.

Presumably, she chose a water route for the family's relocation. In those times, rail travel from Halifax to Massachusetts would have been difficult, for a major passenger train system—the Grand Trunk Railway—did not begin construction in Canada until about 1853.[1] An option for travel was the Cunard steamship fleet. Since the early 1840s it had been under contract with the British Admiralty to carry mail, passengers and freight between Liverpool, England, and Halifax, and on to Boston and New York.[2] Ann and children may have gotten on board such a ship during its Halifax-to-Boston leg—approximately 350 or so nautical miles—and later traveled overland to their destination, Marblehead, Massachusetts, about fifteen-plus miles north of Boston.

Marblehead, with a history of commercial fishing, would be a temporary stop for Ann and at least three of her youngsters before settling in neighboring Salem; Salem is where Ann's brother-in-law Michael Phalen, a tailor, and his wife, Jane Nugent Phalen, and two of their children had moved, either before or not long after Ann's husband, Lawrence, died. (Two more of Michael and Jane's children were born in Salem in June 1848 and September 1849).[3] In Massachusetts, the Phelans presumably became the Phalens, as noted in various records' spelling of the surname.

By today's reckoning, Marblehead and Salem are about three and a half miles apart, close enough for Ann and children to have enjoyed companionship with the other Phalen family members, and near enough for her to receive encouragement and help from them when or if needed. In Marblehead, Ann and her youngsters apparently had to live in separate quarters for a time. The 1850 federal census shows that she and then eight-year-old Michael lived with a family named Buffone, and that eldest daughter Margaret, sixteen, along with ten-year-old brother Edward, were residing in the Eastland family household.[4] In entirely speculative scenarios, two of Ann's girls, daughters Marianne (then about age fourteen) and Ellen (around age five), may have boarded with their aunt and uncle for a time and were not enumerated during a census count. Marianne could have been a help with her young cousins and with housekeeping—again, pure supposition.

More speculation: Ann's daughter Margaret might have been a servant in the Eastland home and may have moved to Marblehead even before her mother emigrated; history tells us that it was not uncommon for young Irish females to leave home and take on such work. Ann, too, once in Marblehead, could have been employed in some way where she was living. Years later, her 1885 death certificate noted her occupation as a nurse.[5] So, while nursing was not yet the formal profession it became, she may have had good instincts and a talent for caring for someone who was chronically ill or aged. It most probably would not have been possible to have all of her children on the premises under such circumstances.

For these new Irish-Americans, there, of course, would have been the everyday tribulations and happy times that any family would experience. The family must have gathered in celebration when Ann's daughter Margaret wed Benjamin Savory March 17, 1853, in Marblehead.[6] The marriage was noted locally in the *Salem Register* on March 28, 1853.[7] The happy news reached Nova Scotia as well in a marriage announcement in Halifax's *Acadian Recorder*.[8]

The earliest substantiated evidence of Ann living in Salem was in 1855, based on a Massachusetts Census report and city directories of that year (the latter sources had been investigated beginning from 1846).[9] The 1855 state census notes that Mary A. (or Maryanne) and Ellen (the two daughters "missing" from Marblehead), and Michael, were living with their mother in Salem. (Edward was not noted, perhaps an error in counting.) Ann and her unmarried children (including Edward) were reported as residing in Salem in the 1860 U.S Census.[10] While Ann's brother-in-law Michael was listed in the 1850 U.S. Census and in the Salem city directory for that year, he was not found in those sources during subsequent years.[11] Perhaps he and his family had returned to Halifax or had moved elsewhere.

Well after Salem's infamous 17th-century witch trials, the community that Ann would come to know was enjoying a far gentler and industrious reputation. Salem was a shipbuilding center into the 19th century and would turn to the production of leather, shoes and textiles when its harbor grew too shallow for maritime enterprises.[12] This was the setting in which Ann raised her family.

As mothers eternal, she must have nursed her young children through childhood diseases, wiped their tears, laughed at their mischief and taken pride in their achievements. It might be that she worked in some sort of nursing capacity to sustain her family—part time, perhaps, when her children were young, and put in more hours later on. Then, with the girls grown into young women, Ann would be waiting for the return of two war-weary sons, Michael William and Edward Augustus, at her home at 66 North in Salem.[13] Life, even in these uncertain times, moved on, as the young men's sister Ellen wed while they were away at war.[14]

chapter VI

THE CIVIL WAR YEARS: 1861-1865

The U.S. Civil War goes down in history as the United States' bloodiest conflict, resulting in deaths due to wounds and disease of between 620,000 and some say possibly 700,000 or more Union and Confederate soldiers.

VI

n April 12, 1861, Confederate forces fired on Fort Sumter, a Union Army military installation located in Charleston Harbor, South Carolina; the two-day bombardment, which saw the fort surrendered to the Confederacy, marked the beginning of the bloody, four-year U.S. Civil War.

Like others in the country, Edward Augustus and Michael William Phalen in Massachusetts would have been paying close attention to news write-ups and conversations about events that had led up to that battle and, after it, President Abraham Lincoln's immediate call for 75,000 military volunteers to help suppress the Southern rebellion.

While there were no radio and TV to spread the news, telegraphed stories in newspapers and probably wildfire-like word of mouth would have kept the brothers and their contemporaries informed. For example, a headline in the *Boston Evening Transcript* newspaper on April 13, 1861, a day after the Fort Sumter assault started, read, "War Begun! The South Strikes the First Blow."[1]

The Phalens would already have known that South Carolina seceded from the Union the previous December, about six weeks after the 1860 election that saw Abraham Lincoln becoming the country's 16th president, and that six other states had seceded from the Union even before Lincoln's March 4, 1861, inauguration. Four more slave states seceded after the Fort Sumter battle. It must have felt to the Phalens that the country in which their family had taken refuge was fractured and in danger of falling apart.

Living in New England, where abolitionist leanings were strong, Edward and Michael likely heard of appearances by speakers such as escaped black slave Frederick Douglass, a leader in the antislavery movement; the

Phalens may have heard rumors about the Underground Railroad, which was thought to be helping Negro slaves to freedom in their own city of Salem and nearby Marblehead.[2] Significant news of the time also circulated around the then-infant Republican Party and its opposition to slavery. The party was founded in the 1850s by activists who opposed both slavery as it existed and the possibility of its gaining momentum in the country's westward expansion. The Republican Party became known for its slogan, "Free soil, free labor, free speech, free men."[3] According to the 1860 U.S. Census, there were four million slaves in the United States.

Still open to debate today, the championing of the Negro slave's freedom threatened the South's agriculture-based economy, primarily cotton production, which depended on slave labor. For this and other reasons, historians suggest, Southerners did not want to see newcomer Republicans, with their abolitionist leanings, gaining a foothold in American politics: That is exactly what happened when Lincoln became the nation's first Republican president.

The 1860 U.S. Census identified about four million foreigners living in the United States, of whom 1.6 million were from Ireland. Most of them lived in crowded urban areas such as Boston, Philadelphia and New York City, and among them were people who were having their own worries about abolitionism; they feared not being able to earn a living if slavery were eradicated. Civil War scholar and author Christian G. Samito writes:

"The prospect of millions of freed slaves migrating north and competing for already scarce labor alarmed workers barely able to support their families. While white Irish lived in misery in Boston's slums and exhausted themselves in securing a livelihood, they viewed free blacks not with empathy as another wronged group but as a threat to their jobs and tenuous social position."[4]

Along with economic worries, the Irish—especially Irish Catholics— were the targets of prejudice, largely because of opposition in the United States to the so-called "Church of Rome." Signs reading "No Irish Need Apply" were often placed at the doors of factories, stores, farms and other places of employment.[5]

And yet, despite the anti-Irish climate of the times, Edward and Michael were willing to fight for their adopted country. Shortly after Lincoln's April 15, 1861, call for volunteer militia troops to suppress the Confederate insurrection, they voluntarily enlisted in the Union Army. They were among an estimated one hundred and fifty thousand Irishmen in the North who fought for the Union during the Civil War.[6]

chapter VII

THE FIGHTING IRISH

The Irish in America had a strong presence in the U.S. Civil War. This Gettysburg Battlefield monument with Celtic cross and symbolic wolfhound honors New York units of the legendary Civil War Irish Brigade. Pennsylvania and Massachusetts regiments also were part of the Irish Brigade. Photo courtesy of Russell Recchion.

VII

hile they joined military units composed of men with many eth-
nic backgrounds, the Irish distinguished themselves as valorous
in organizations made up primarily of those of Irish heritage,
such as the famous Irish Brigade[1]; it was composed of the 63rd New York
Infantry Regiment; the 69th New York Infantry Regiment (the Fighting
69th); the 88th New York Infantry Regiment; the 116th Regiment, Pennsylvania Volunteer Infantry; and the 28th Massachusetts Volunteer Infantry Regiment. Michael William Phalen became part of another predomi-
nantly Irish unit, the Ninth Regiment Massachusetts Volunteer Infantry.

Writes Christian G. Samito:

"Few expected an enthusiastic Irish-American response when Lincoln
called for volunteers to help quash the rebellion after the South fired on
Fort Sumter. After all, they had opposed Lincoln and denounced reform;
they had remained loyal to the Democratic Party, and had supported the
South and the institution of slavery. However, many Irish in the North remained patriotic citizens of their adopted land, devoted to the Union and
to the Constitution that governed it."[2]

Brothers Edward Augustus and Michael William Phalen could have
been among those Irish in the North who were devoted to the Union. After all, they had been brought to this country when they were very young
children and had grown up as Americans and, if not as formal citizens, as
part of the fiber of the land.

Author Susannah Ural Bruce speaks of multiple possible reasons the
Irish in America were willing to take up arms: "For some Irish men, especially the radical Irish nationalists in America known as the Fenians,
military service offered experience they could apply to their anticipated

war for an independent Ireland. Others referred to the opportunities they had found in America and spoke of their hope to save the Union as an asylum for future Irish refugees. Some served to challenge nativist prejudice and prove their loyalty as Americans, hoping their sacrifices would lead to new opportunities in postwar America. For other Irishmen, military service was not necessarily based on ideology or heritage, but rather on a basic need for the money, clothing, food, and shelter they could earn in the Union Army, though at a tremendous risk."[3]

Union privates at the beginning of the war earned thirteen dollars a month.[4] On top of that, there were incentives of cash bonuses, or bounties, from the federal government and states. For example, in July of 1861 Congress authorized a $100 bounty fee to men enlisting for three years.[5]

Citing information from an 1862 issue of the Irish-oriented Boston newspaper, the *Pilot*, Bruce notes that the city of Boston was giving a $100 bounty for volunteers, and that the total of bounties, salaries and allowances, such as for time served, amounted to $555; this, "at nearly a full year's salary, was quite an incentive for the average unskilled Irish laborer," she writes. Adds Bruce: "The catch, of course, was that over half that amount depended upon his survival, but for many men, the benefits outweighed the risks."[6]

While it had been used in previous U.S. conflicts to increase manpower, the program of enticing enlistees into the army with cash bounties became abusive during the Civil War. With troop numbers waning, Congress passed the Enrollment Act of 1863 (a conscription or draft law); it awarded three-year enlistees $300 and five-year recruits $400, which were divided up and paid in monthly installments with the soldiers' regular compensation.[7] But it was what happened at the state and local levels, due to the law's having charged states with enlistee quotas, that spun bounties out of control.

The "War Department assigned each congressional district a quota based on a percentage of its eligible males minus the number of men who had already served in the army," explains historian James M. McPherson. "But each district was given fifty days to fill this quota with volunteers. Drafting would be resorted to for only the number of men short of the quota. State and local officials used all the means at their command to secure sufficient volunteers to escape the stigma of conscription." McPherson says that bounties were the principal means of stimulating volunteering.[8]

The problem: Wealthier districts were attracting new volunteers from poorer districts by often paying them more than $1,000 to enlist. This led to widespread bounty-jumping, wherein men were enlisting to collect a hefty bonus, then deserting from the service and doing the same thing over again in other districts. The bounty practice was later outlawed with passage of the Selective Service Act of 1917.[9]

Also problematic was the 1863 Enrollment Act's provision that a man who was drafted could either find someone who would take his place in the army (substitution) or pay a commutation fee of $300 that exempted him from that particular draft. Substitution also had been allowed in the Confederate Army, notes McPherson. Of the situation in the North, he writes, "Veteran volunteers who were risking their lives resented a system that permitted others to buy their way out of the risk."[10]

In addition, he states, "The privilege of hiring a substitute or paying a $300 commutation fee to escape the draft also provoked working-class resentment. Since $300 represented more than half a year's wages for an unskilled workingman, the cry arose (as it had in the South a year earlier) that this practice made it a rich man's war and a poor man's fight."[11] In 1864, Congress abolished the commutation privilege, except for conscientious objectors.[12]

THE PHALEN BOYS

Whatever their reasons for joining the Union Army, brothers Michael William Phalen and Edward Augustus Phalen did so, and with distinction. Their stories follow.

chapter VIII

Michael William Phalen

This picture of Michael William Phalen in military uniform was taken in 1864, shortly after he was mustered out of the Union Army. The photo was shot at J.J. Hawes, Photographers, on Tremont Row in Boston. The young Michael was in good company, for Josiah Johnson Hawes was a noted photographer who took portrait photos of many illuminaries, including Henry Wadsworth Longfellow and Daniel Webster.

Chaplain Thomas Scully celebrates Mass with men of the Ninth Regiment Massa-chusetts Volunteer Infantry at Camp Cass, Arlington Heights, Virginia, in 1861. Civil War-era photo courtesy of the Library of Congress.

VIII

The firing on Fort Sumter by the Confederates "caused a thrill of surprise in every patriotic heart," wrote Union Army veteran Daniel George Macnamara in his personal chronicle of the Civil War. "Everywhere could be seen then the young men, and the middle-aged, ready and anxious to don a uniform and shoulder a musket in order to fight for the 'old flag' and the preservation of the Union. Patriotism and love of country was as publicly prominent in the voices and hearts of the Irish-American citizens as it was in the native born. All vied with each other in their feverish haste to volunteer, and go at once to the seat of war, that they might boast in future years how they had a hand in putting down the rebellion."[1]

At age nineteen, Michael William Phalen of Salem, Massachusetts, was working in the tanning trade. Likely caught up in the patriotic "feverish haste" Macnamara described, he volunteered for the Union Army. The law required those between eighteen and twenty to obtain parental permission to enlist.[2] But as a friend in later years recounted, Michael gave "his age as twenty-one, lest on account of his youth he should fail to be accepted."[3] It is not difficult to imagine what mother Ann Phalen's reaction might have been when she found out what he had done. She would have both sons, Edward and Michael, in harm's way.

If Michael was bound and determined to be on the front line of action, he would forge that determination into a quality that was admired by his commander and others. He is mentioned in complimentary terms in the book Macnamara wrote, "The History of the Ninth Regiment, Massachusetts Volunteer Infantry, June 1861-June 1864." Likewise Irish, Macnamara served with Michael in the Ninth Regiment Massachusetts Volunteer

Infantry. One of three brothers who enlisted in the Ninth, Macnamara became a first lieutenant and regimental quartermaster. His book, first published in 1899, provides poignant evidence of what he, Michael and the men of the Ninth endured during their years in the epic war.[4]

After a period of training, Michael was mustered into the Union Army on June 11, 1861, as a first sergeant in the Ninth's Company F. The regiment, one-thousand and twenty-two men, according to Macnamara, came to be known as "the Fighting Ninth," and also "the Fighting Irish." It was made up primarily of soldiers of Irish Catholic heritage who either had been born in Ireland, or who, like Michael, were of Irish descent. He would receive recognition over time for his steadfastness in the midst of battle and his dedication, and he was promoted accordingly. He was commissioned second lieutenant, September 7, 1861; first lieutenant, January 28, 1862; and appointed regimental adjutant, August 28, 1862.[5]

Michael was injured in at least two engagements: the Battle of Gaines' Mill in Virginia, June 27, 1862, where he received a wound to the forehead from a piece of shell; and the Battle of Mine Run in Virginia, November 27, 1863, where he was struck on a hip by an unexploded and ricocheting shell.[6] Although hurt, he chose to remain on both battlefields, taking time out only for the "time required to dress his wounds," as a compatriot would later state.[7]

Why such bravery? It may be that Michael, like others of Irish heritage, joined the Union Army for one or more of a cluster of reasons—ranging from possible economic need, to mixed feelings about how emancipation of the slaves would affect the livelihoods of Irish in America, to proving that the Irish were as loyal Americans as those who were native-born. It would seem that Michael's actions during the brutal Civil War war defined his loyalty to his adopted country. In later years, a military comrade would say of Michael: "He was with his regiment in every engagement. Neatness, precision and order characterized him in the discharge of details of his office; everything was in its proper place and attended to at the proper time. His exertion and example, his promptitude and fidelity to duty went far towards creating that discipline and good name for his regiment of which we were all so proud."[8]

THE "FIGHTING NINTH"

The Ninth Massachusetts was organized by Boston businessman Thomas Cass. Born in Ireland, Cass had been a captain and commander

of a largely Irish-American Massachusetts volunteer militia called the Columbian Artillery. Responding to Lincoln's call for volunteers, Cass, with
the approval of Massachusetts Governor John Albion Andrew, set about
recruiting men for a new Irish-American fighting unit during April and
May of 1861; originally the Thirteenth Massachusetts Volunteer Militia,
it became the Ninth Regiment Massachusetts Volunteer Infantry, com-
manded by Colonel Cass. The recruitment efforts drew ten companies of
men—six from Boston and one each from Milford, Marlboro, Stoughton
and Salem, Michael's hometown.[9]

Early on, the recruits were housed in temporary barracks in Boston's
Faneuil Hall. The historic setting, with colonial-era meeting rooms, once
resounded with talk of the Boston Tea Party and years later was the site
of abolitionist speeches against slavery before and during the Civil War.[10]
Macnamara remembered that the close confinement of the men in Faneuil
Hall was "very irksome" and the accommodations "quite unsatisfactory."
But, as they waited to move on to new training grounds, some good did
come out of being quartered there, he reflected: "In the meantime, and
in order to give the men some good exercise, the colonel ordered all the
companies to assemble on Boston Common for drill each evening. These
outings were productive of great good, both in drill and exercise, and in
aiding to keep the men in good health and spirits."[11]

Michael apparently took the drills to heart, for he became adept at the
precise routine of handling a musket, as noted in a manual of arms. His
prowess is described by Macnamara, who recalled a time that Michael's
Company F, men from Salem, marched into Faneuil Hall to the martial
music of fife and drum. "Company F was received with cheers which lasted
several minutes. After a short rest, the 1st sergeant, Michael W. Phalen,
gave an exhibition drill in company movements. All the evolutions were
well executed, and received great applause from the young soldier specta-
tors. The manual of arms was well done and brought much praise to the
instructor, Sergeant Phalen."[12]

So prevalent was war fever at the time, that young boys were trying to
enlist in the army, according to Macnamara. Those "who were refused on
account of their juvenile appearance, would climb the spout outside Faneuil Hall, and get into the window at the risk of falling some twenty feet
to the sidewalk," he remembered. Finally, guards had to be stationed at
windows to "prevent these incorrigible youngsters from forcing their way
into the hall."[13]

On May 12, 1861, the men of the Ninth were put on the steamer Nellie Baker and taken to Long Island in Boston Harbor to advance their training at Camp Wightman, named in honor of Boston Mayor Joseph Wightman.[14] The Ninth was the first regiment to be quartered on the island, which in the past had been home to colonial-era planters.[15]

Macnamara wrote of that day: "The transference of the regiment from Faneuil Hall to Long Island, was, indeed, a great blessing to all parties interested. The freedom of the island, with its green fields, pure salt air and bright sky, infused new life into both officers and men. The camp of wall tents was well laid out, and presented a clean and spacious appearance; and, as it was situated towards the south shore of the island, ample room was given for a fine, grassy parade and drill ground."[16]

And drill and march Michael and the others would, in "incessant rounds from day to day," noted Macnamara. While rough on them, he indicated, "It seemed as though no one could get enough of it." The men were eager to become skilled at handling the "old sixty-nine calibre, buck and ball muzzle-loading musket," he said.[17]

On Sundays, the men could look forward to visits from relatives and friends, wives or sweethearts, Macnamara recalled. "As time wore on each Sunday was deemed to be our last on Long Island, and when the hour arrived in the evening for the departure of our visitors to the city, many affecting farewells took place as though for the last time," he wrote. "The strong hand-shake, the fervid 'good-bye,' and 'God bless you' of the men; and the kiss, the smile and the tear of the women, as if for the final parting, made these departures more depressing and sad than our young, light-hearted Irish-American soldiers would wish to know."[18]

It might be that mom Ann Phalen and Michael's sisters came to visit on one of those Sundays. And maybe, Ellen J. Fay, a young woman who was born in Ireland, also dropped by. Just when a romance was kindled is lost in time, but she would become Michael's wife. Romantic speculation conjures a wedding on the one-day furlough the regiment was granted before departing for war.[19]

Macnamara recounted an event that signaled the men would soon be leaving Long Island. "The arrival of new gray uniforms, of good material, muskets, equipments [sic], etc., served to warn us that the day of our departure for the seat of war was drawing near." (How satisfactory those gray uniforms were would become a matter of debate.) In late June of 1861, the regiment, men in uniforms, "armed and equipped," boarded a steamer to

Long Wharf in Boston, where Colonel Cass was to go to the State House for an official ceremony and receive the Massachusetts flag from Governor Andrew.

Macnamara described the event as celebratory, with the men greeted by throngs of cheering and clapping people and bands playing as they marched and stood before the State House. There, the governor expressed thanks to Cass as commander, and through him, the "splendid regiment."

Macnamara noted that the governor further told Cass: "I understand, sir, that, like yourself, a majority, if not nearly all of your command, derive their origin, either by birth or directly by descent, from another country than this. As religion makes no distinction in the human family, so the United States of America knows no distinction between its native born citizens and those born in other countries. ... To you and all your soldiers, from all the inhabitants of this land today begins an indebtedness which it will take long to discharge, and by future generations will you be remembered."

As the state flag was received, a regimental color guard displayed two gifts of silk banners: the red, white and blue of the Stars and Stripes and another in green symbolizing Irish pride and courage. In his introduction to Macnamara's book, Christian G. Samito explains: "Flags provided a symbolic link between the soldiers and the Bay State communities they left behind." Friends delivered a federal banner, and the widow of ex-Mayor Harrison Gray Otis donated a magnificent green silk Irish flag to the Ninth Massachusetts before it departed for Washington.[20] The latter flag, carried in battle and tattered from war, is today housed at the Massachusetts State House Hall of Flags.

On one side of the green flag in a scroll of gold letters was written "Thy Sons By Adoption, Thy Firm Supporters and Defenders From Duty, Affection and Choice." In gold letters as well were the words, "Presented to Col. Thomas Cass, 9th Regiment, Massachusetts Irish Volunteers." At the flag's center was the American coat of arms, the eagle and shield. On the reverse side was the Irish harp, whose strings, in ground color, denoted the 'Red, White and Blue,' surmounted by thirty-four stars, surrounded by a wreath of shamrocks. Over the harp was the legend, "As aliens and strangers thou didst us befriend. As sons and true patriots we do thee defend." Below the harp were two wolf dogs, emblematic of Ireland, and the motto, "Gentle When Stroked, Fierce When Provoked." Underneath it all was this declarative motto: "The Union Must Be Preserved."[21]

Notes Samito: "To the men of the Ninth Massachusetts in the field, the emerald banner served as a dual symbol of remembrance of Ireland and service to their new country."[22]

The Ninth's men not only would have an Irish flag to buoy their spirits during wartime; for much of the Civil War they had a Catholic priest, or chaplain, traveling with them, to tend to their spiritual needs. One of those chaplains—the first—was Rev. Thomas Scully. Mustered into the Ninth June 17, 1861, he had been captured by the Confederates on two occasions, escaping the first time and released unconditionally the second time by his captors when seriously ill with malaria.[23] He resigned his commission October 31, 1862.[24]

chapter IX

Into The Battle

First Lieut. Adjutant Michael W. Phalen (top row, far right) stands next to his commander, Col. Patrick R. Guiney, in this 1863 group shot of Ninth Regiment Massachusetts Volunteer Infantry officers at an encampment at Culpeper, Virginia. Seated, bottom row, left to right are: 2nd Lt. William A. Plunkett; 1st Lt. Daniel G. Macnamara; 1st Lt. William R. Bourke; (ink smeared, possibly 1st Lt. James O'Donnell or Lt. Col. Cronwell G. Rowell); and 1st Lt. Timothy Dacy (or possibly Deasy). Standing, left to right are: Capt. Timothy R. Bourke; Capt. Martin O'Brien; Capt. Michael Flynn; 1st Lt. Patrick E. Murphy; 1st Lt. Bernard F. Finan; Surgeon James F. Sullivan; Col. Guiney; and Adjutant Phalen. Photo courtesy of Mass. Commandery MOLLUS/U.S. Army Heritage and Education Center, Carlisle, Pennsylvania.

IX

n June 25, 1861, a day after the State House ceremonies, more than one thousand men of the Ninth left for war duty. They boarded three steamers and sailed south along the East Coast, entered Chesapeake Bay and the Potomac River, disembarked at Washington, D.C., on June 29th, 1861, and were being greeted the next morning by President Abraham Lincoln.[1] Whatever Michael W. Phalen's feelings might have been about Lincoln and his desire to free the slaves, this event must have seemed quite a send-off for the young soldier—an event that put him in the center of history in the making.

How well-equipped for war the men of the Ninth were was on the minds of enlisted men and commanders alike. An enlisted man's view is brought to life with wry honesty in the diary of Corporal Timothy J. Regan, a member of the Ninth. In his August 21, 1861, diary entry, he penned: "Today the Quartermaster issued the United States regulation uniform, and we have laid aside the grey suits which we brought from home and in which we were sometimes mistaken for rebels."[2] He later would write in a December 13, 1861, entry: "The State of Massachusetts has sent us a bill for the grey uniform furnished us when we left home; each man is charged thirty five dollars and ninety two and a half cents which is more than twice what the regulation uniform furnished by the United States cost, and the regulation uniform is ten times better."[3]

Massachusetts Governor Andrew's parting comment that "the United States of America knows no distinction between its native-born citizens and those born in other countries" apparently wore thin in the actual war. In "The Harp and The Eagle," historian Susannah Ural Bruce speaks of Irish commanders who "indicated that while native-born Americans may have appreciated the abilities of Irishmen on the battlefield or during camp festivities, such sentiments disappeared when it came to supplying and supporting Irish regiments."

Bruce pointed to Colonel Cass, commander of the Ninth, as early on having been dissatisfied with Massachusetts' support of the Irish volunteers. Bruce says Cass voiced his concerns to Governor Andrew during the first summer of the war, noting that other regiments had benefited from tremendous funds from donations of Boston's wealthy, while his regiment was sent only a third of what other regiments received and "were expected to provide their own arms and uniforms."[4]

THE INFANTRYMAN: FIGHTING A WAR ON FOOT

The Ninth, part of the Second Brigade, First Division, Fifth Corps, was assigned to the Army of the Potomac, which had two goals: to guard Washington, D.C., against a Confederate invasion, and to defeat the Confederate Army of Northern Virginia.[5] As an infantryman, Michael was a member of what historians have called the backbone of an army. "Despite the cavalry's glamour and the artillery's power, the infantry was by far the most important branch of Civil War armies," writes scholar James M. McPherson. "The infantry inflicted and suffered 80 to 90 percent of the battle casualties."[6] Macnamara described the conditions under which the infantry foot soldier labored as often marching through rain-soaked areas, with clay-like mud that stuck to "an army shoe like a brother."[7]

After rough military encounters and often marches that were many miles long, Michael and the others would spend nights seeking rest in bivouac conditions, sleeping outdoors, at times on damp ground, with little or no shelter. The regiment "marched, bivouacked and battled for three years at the front, in the Army of the Potomac, during its campaigns in Virginia, Maryland and Pennsylvania," noted Macnamara.[8] "It was no child's play to carry a musket, a well-filled knapsack, a haversack containing three days' rations, a canteen full of water, and equipments [sic] with forty rounds of buck and ball cartridges, aggregating a weight of forty pounds or more per man."[9]

The men of the Ninth were in force at battles with names that ring out across history. They include, among others: Mechanicsville (Mechanicsville, Virginia) June 26, 1862; Gaines' Mill (Hanover County, Virginia), June 27, 1862; Malvern Hill (Henrico County, Virginia), July 1, 1862; Manassas, or Second Bull Run (Manassas, Virginia), August 29-30; Antietam, (Sharpsburg, Maryland), September 17-18, 1862; Fredericksburg (Fredericksburg, Virginia), December 13-14, 1862; Chancellorsville (Spotsylvania County, Virginia), May 3-5, 1863; Gettysburg (Adams County, Pennsylvania), July 2-3, 1863; Mine Run (Orange County, Virginia), November 27-30, 1863; the Wilderness (forest on a bank of the Rapidan River, beyond Chancellorsville, Virginia), May 5-7, 1864.[10] (See related section, *Addendum: A Memorial for a Civil War Veteran* for additional battles in which the Ninth participated.)

The late-19th-century Civil War analyses and statistics of William F. Fox are still quoted by historians. He reported that the Fifth Corps, which included the Ninth Regiment, was famous for its prominent roles in the battles of Gaines' Mill [during which Michael was injured] and Malvern Hill, during which the commander, Colonel Cass, was mortally wounded. Fox wrote of the Ninth in terms of bravery, describing it as "An Irish regiment, whose gallant service on many fields attested the oft-acknowledged valor of the Irish soldier." Of Gaines' Mill, he commented: "The Ninth distinguished itself at Gaines' Mill by the steadiness with which it sustained a heavy attack, its losses that day amounting to 57 killed, 149 wounded and 25 missing; total 231."[11] Macnamara, meanwhile, put the Ninth's Gaines' Mill losses at 252.[12]

Overall, of those who fought at Gaines' Mill, Union casualties were 6,837 (of whom 894 were killed; 3,114 wounded; 2,829 captured); the Confederacy's casualties totaled 7,993 (of whom 1,483 were killed; 6,402 wounded; 108 missing).[13]

Although wounded in this battle, Michael stayed and fought with the troops. A few days later, he was participating in the Battle of Malvern Hill, July 1, 1862, another bloodbath. On this day, Colonel Cass suffered mortal wounds of his face and mouth.[14] He died eleven days later at his home in Boston.[15] Macnamara cited 166 as the the total number of men in the Ninth who were wounded and killed at Malvern Hill.[16] Of those who fought at Malvern Hill, Union casualties were 3,007 (of whom 314 were killed; 1,875 wounded; and 818 missing). Confederate casualties were 5,650 (of whom 869 were killed; 4,241 wounded; 540 missing).[17]

Years later, Michael eloquently recalled an incident that took place during the Battle of Malvern Hill. His comments, which follow, were included in Macnamara's book.

"At the battle of Malvern Hill, the right wing separated from the left, taking the colors with them, and went forward joining the left of the 44th

New York. After advancing a considerable distance, and when we were about ready to retire, Acting Lieut. John F. Doherty was wounded in the leg. On retiring with the colors, we were under an oblique fire from the enemy. Lieutenant Flaherty was on Doherty's left and I was on his right, all facing to the rear. This brought me on the danger side of Doherty which he immediately recognized and refused to go a step farther until I had taken a position on the left; thus exposing himself to the fire and shielding us, claiming, in his most vehement manner, that as he was wounded and therefore useless for further service, the best use he could make of himself was as a bulwark or protection to us who were not wounded. Bearing in mind the surroundings and the fact that there was great uncertainty whether any of us would safely reach the rear, and that there was no one to applaud his speech or his conduct, this incident has always held a prominent place in my memory as one of the rare instances of true bravery."[18]

Michael did not laud his own bravery during that conflict. A companion who had served with him in the Ninth later said of Michael: "Phalen distinguished himself by conspicuous gallantry in the battle of Malvern Hill."[19] Michael was fighting there just four days after he was wounded in the forehead.

A New Commander

After the death of Cass, Colonel Patrick R. Guiney would take over as commander of the Ninth. Born in Ireland, he was a young Boston lawyer and married with a child when he served in the Civil War.[20]

Michael's name appears on different occasions in a book composed of letters that Guiney, his commander, wrote home to his wife, "Jennie," from out in the field. Writer Christian G. Samito discovered those letters in the Dinand Library Rare Book Room at Massachusetts' College of the Holy Cross. Along with an explanatory historical narrative by Samito, the often emotionally charged missives are published in "Commanding Boston's Irish Ninth: The Civil War Letters of Colonel Patrick R. Guiney, Ninth Massachusetts Volunteer Infantry." [21]

While offering personal insights into how Guiney, as a man away from his family, was coping with the exigencies of war, the letters also provide glimpses into Michael's life and character. Unlike some who joined the Ninth out of the fear that emancipated slaves would ultimately take jobs from Irish-Americans in the North, Guiney, as an educated lawyer, apparently had no such worry; and his antislavery beliefs did not sit well with some in the regiment, writes Samito. "Guiney openly expressed his sentiments, and these political views and support for Lincoln caused him trouble with the Ninth Massachusetts." One such trouble occurred when Guiney assumed command of the Ninth and became the object of a "conspiracy" of eleven officers, led by Captain Timothy O'Leary, who wanted him replaced. "The clique sent a petition to Massachusetts Governor Andrew criticizing Guiney for his absence from the battle of Malvern Hill on July 1, 1862," Samito notes. "They ignored the fact that, at the time, Guiney was extremely ill with malaria which rendered him unable to move without help and confined him to an ambulance."[22]

Macnamara recalled Guiney's illness in his book. "Lieutenant-Colonel Guiney, who had been prostrated since the close of the battle of the 27th ult., had previously been taken violently sick on the field, and had to be assisted to an ambulance. From lack of proper food, medicine and rest, he was so weak as to finally be unable to move without assistance. The surgeon pronounced him sick with malarial fever and ordered him home. Colonel Cass ordered Captain O'Leary of Company F in charge of the left wing of the regiment, as acting major."[23] After Cass fell on the battlefield and the subsequent wounding of another officer, O'Leary assumed temporary command of the regiment; he had to relinquish it to Guiney when the now-colonel returned to the field the first week of August 1862.[24] On August 6, 1862, a day after he arrived at Harrison's Landing, Virginia, Guiney wrote his wife, telling her of the welcome he had from his troops—men he said gave him "the heartiest and loudest welcome." He also wrote of the malicious, savage and morose stance of many of the officers who had sided against him. "The officers had written a most slanderous communication to Governor Andrew about me. I pronounced them liars to their teeth."[25]

Michael, then a first lieutenant, was one of the eleven officers who had complained about Guiney.[26] Interestingly, according to Samito's meticulous research, Father Thomas Scully contacted the governor of Massachusetts early in September 1862 and communicated the following: "The regiment is going on well. Our new colonel is very much beloved by the men and most of those foolish officers who signed their names to that infamous libel have apologized and are prepared at any time to do so publicly."[27]

By September 19, 1862, all but two of the eleven officers had recanted their complaint to the governor. Michael Phalen was one of the nine who had regretted their complaint and stated that no action of Guiney's would justify an accusation of cowardice.[28] It would seem that Guiney held no malice against Michael for having been among those who had written about him to the governor on July 31, 1862. For one thing, Michael was appointed adjutant the following month, on August 28th. (Ironically, according to Samito's research, it was as adjutant in October of 1863 that Michael, in another matter, charged Captain O'Leary, who had led the "coup" against Guiney, with conduct unbecoming an officer and a gentleman.)[29]

chapter X

Proving His Mettle

This granite monument at the Gettysburg Civil War battlefield honors the Ninth Regiment Massachusetts Volunteer Infantry for its role in holding an area called Big Round Top. Photo courtesy of the National Park Service.

Head Quarters 9th Mass Vols.
Jan 13. 1863

Phalen, Michael W.
1st Lieut & Adgt.

applies for Leave of Absence

Hd. Qrs. 9th Mass. Vols.
Jan. 13. 1863

Respectfully forwarded &
recommended. Lt. Phalen
is an efficient and zealous
officer, and although wound-
-ed at the battle of Gaines
Mill, he remained with
the regiment and assist-
-ed me very in the re-
-organization of this command
after the Peninsular campaign
If the exigencies of the service
will permit, he ought to be
allowed this privilege.
P. R. Guiney Col
Comdg. 9th Mass.

In recommending that leave be granted to Michael William Phalen, Col. Patrick R. Guiney, commander of the Ninth Regiment Massachusetts Volunteer Infantry, notes Phalen's having remained on the battlefield, despite being wounded during the Civil War Battle of Gaines' Mill.

X

Being an adjutant was a demanding position and one of respon-
sibility, according to Macnamara: "The main line of work in an
infantry regiment devolves on the colonel, the adjutant, the sergeant-major and the 1st sergeants of the companies. The orders, standing
and otherwise, of the colonel are enough to keep these officers busy from
early morning to night."[1] How Michael in particular comported himself
as adjutant was made a matter of record in Macnamara's book. "Adjutant
Phalen, who was second to none in his duties, attended diligently to everything pertaining to his office, aided by the sergeant-major of the non-
commissioned staff."[2]

An official January 1863 letter recommending that Michael be granted a
request for leave is an indication of Col. Patrick R. Guiney's positive feelings
about his adjutant. "Respectfully forwarded and recommended. Lt. Phalen
is an efficient and zealous officer, and although wounded at the battle of
Gaines Mill, he remained with the regiment and assisted me very _____
in the reorganization of this command after the Peninsular Campaign. If the
exigencies of the service will permit, he ought to be allowed this privilege."[3]
Major General George Gordon Meade, who later would be given command
of the Army of the Potomac, approved the time off.[4]

Michael's original request to Guiney follows.[5]

Head Quarters 9th Mass. Vols.
Camp near Falmouth, Va.
Jan. 14, 63
Colonel:
I respectfully request leave of absence for ten (10) days.

> *The necessity of transacting business of much importance to me per-*
> *sonally, and the natural desire to visit my family, no member of which I*
> *have seen for nearly two years, causes me to make this request which I*
> *earnestly hope you will consider intitled [sic] to a favorable consideration.*
> *I have the honor to be*
> *Very Respectfully*
> *Your_____*
> *Michael W. Phalen*
> *1st Lieut & Adjt 9th Mass Vols*

That Guiney thought well of Michael is evident in references to him in the letters the colonel wrote home to his wife, Jennie. For example, in one written on May 8, 1863, he discussed another officer's choices for who should or should not be promoted to major. "I stick to the Adjutant [Michael Phalen]—he is the best man," Guiney wrote.[6] No evidence has surfaced that Michael was actually up for such a promotion, and Guiney's comment may have been wishful thinking about someone he realized had proven merit.

Two days later, in an official report dated May 10, 1863, Guiney thanked Michael and six other officers, non-commissioned officers and men of various companies for their "meritorious service" during the Battle of Chancellorsville, (May 3-5, 1863). As part of the duties of his position as adjutant, "Adjutant M.W. Phalen" signed Guiney's report. It was read to the men of the Ninth at a dress parade, Macnamara noted in his book.[7]

A day short of a week later, on May 16, 1863, Guiney would be writing Jennie about the personal tragedy that had fallen upon his adjutant, the death of Michael's wife, Ellen [J. Fay] Phalen. "The Adjutant's wife is dead—he is gone home. He felt dreadfully at the sad news," Guiney penned.[8] An obituary printed May 18, 1863, in the *Salem Register* noted that Ellen had died May 14, 1863, "at the residence of her brother," John E. Fay, in Boston.[9] State of Massachusetts Vital Records, meanwhile, note her official date of death as May 15, 1863, and a City of Boston death registry recorded the cause of her death as a "Sore Throat" of two months' duration.[10]

Michael had received a telegram informing him of his wife's death and requested emergency leave. Guiney approved the leave and recommended to a higher up that it be granted, as a personal favor to him. To that other officer, Michael had written a brief request containing poignant language that echoes over time: "I respectfully request leave of absence for ten days to visit Boston, Mass. The enclosed telegram furnishes my reasons."[11]

It is not difficult to put oneself in the place of Michael, empathize with his sadness, and imagine the comforting he would have received from mother Ann Phalen and his siblings back in Massachusetts as he grieved; their concern for him as he went back to the scene of war must have seemed palpable. He did not stay long in Boston. On May 21, 1863, another *Salem Register* article, under the headline "War and Incidents," stated that Michael Phalen had been home for "a day or two" after his wife's death and returned to his regiment on May 20, 1863.[12]

Back on the battlefront, Michael continued to gain the respect of his commander. Guiney, in a June 25, 1863, letter to Jennie from camp at Aldie, Virginia, referred to Michael's dependability. While others were out sick, he wrote, "myself and the Adjutant are, as usual, doing the business."[13]

One senses a camaraderie in the men's relationship, for Michael is mentioned in casual references in Guiney's letters. For example, Guiney seemed only half-miffed when he wrote Jennie the following on August 15, 1863. "Your stamps were also received in good order, but [Captain Michael] Flynn and the Adjutant [Michael Phalen] stole them from me right off. So I shall have to borrow one of my own to put on this letter."[14]

While Michael had remained with the regiment after being wounded at the Battle of Mine Run in November of 1863, he began to feel the effects of his injury a few days later and requested sick leave. A surgeon's report stated: "Adjutant M.W. Phalen of this Regiment having applied to me for a certificate on which to ground an application for leave of absence I do hereby certify that I have carefully examined this officer and find him suffering with subacute inflammation in the left iliac region, accompanied with pain upon motion, tenderness and soreness, caused by contusion by a solid (partially spent) shell received on Friday, Nov. 27th in the last battle across the Rapidan [River], which renders him unfit for duty. I further certify that, in my opinion, this officer will not be fit for duty in a less period than twenty days. Given at camp near Bealton, Virginia, this sixth day of December, 1863."[15]

Guiney gave swift approval, again noting Michael's behavior of staying on the battlefield though wounded, and by December 12, 1863, Fifth Corps headquarters granted the twenty-day sick leave to Boston.[16] Michael could be home for Christmas, recuperating with his family in neighboring Salem.

Macnamara provided an account of Michael's having been wounded at

Mine Run, including comments about the adjutant's bravery in his own words and in colorful language delivered by two soldiers:

"While in the line of battle our adjutant, M.W. Phalen, was hit by an un-exploded, ricocheting, spent spherical shell, on the hip. The shock lamed him considerably without any other apparent serious damage. He remained on the field, but was unable to perform any physical duty for a few days. One of the Ninth men declared that 'Our adjutant was too good a soldier to leave the field, even if he was hit by a cannon ball!' Another man forcibly remarked: 'When Adjutant Phalen was a lieutenant commanding our company at Gaines' Mill fight, he was hit in the forehead and bleeding, and then, bedad! he wouldn't go to the rear. He called it a mere scratch. The wound looked then, for all the world, like a red cross in the centre [sic] of his forehead.'"[17]

From a letter that Colonel Guiney wrote to his wife on April 5, 1864, it appears that he, like those soldiers Macnamara mentioned in his book, saw Michael as a man one could count on. He wrote:

"Poor [Lieut. Col. Patrick T.] Hanley is sick again. Lucky time! Just as campaign is about to open. He is going to Washington, and I shall be alone again in battle except the Adjt.—who, as usual, is worth all the rest put together." That same letter implies that Michael, along with the surgeon and the chaplain, enjoyed a warm relationship with Guiney and a cordial one with his wife. "Our friends are well and the Dr. [Sullivan], Father Egan, Adjt. [Phalen] etc frequently speak of you and wish to be remembered to you."[18]

A DAY FOR THE IRISH

Christian G. Samito's research shows that Guiney's daughter, Louise, or "Loolie," who grew up to be a poet, remembered a time when she and her mother had visited the Ninth's winter quarters and she played with Adjutant Phalen's two spaniels.[19] The colonel's wife was on hand when the Ninth celebrated St. Patrick's Day March 17, 1863.[20]

Michael displayed a fun-loving side on this day, when he and another gentleman were in charge of the festivities. Included were horse racing; a sack race; a race for a greased pig; climbing a 15-foot-high greased pole, with the prize of a ten-day furlough to the one who got to the top (no one was able to do so); a mock dress parade, and more. Macnamara, himself a first lieutenant at the time, recalled that day and how looking forward to it had charged up the men's spirits:

"The anticipation of the coming sport on the 17th acted as a leaven to the lethargy that permeated the soldiers of the army to a more or less extent. The light-heartedness that was now visible throughout the Ninth Massachusetts was contagious and very soon affected the rank and file of the 62nd Pennsylvania, who were in winter quarters near us. They too looked forward to a jolly time with their old friends of the Ninth. Adjutant M.W. Phalen and Quartermaster [Thomas] Mooney were given full charge of the entertainments."[21]

Tragically, Mooney, who was one of the riders in the horse racing event, collided with another horse and rider. Mooney died of head injuries ten days later. "This sad affair put a damper on the races, which were shortly discontinued," wrote Macnamara, who would take Mooney's place as quartermaster.[22]

But during the regiment's intermittent periods of waiting to be thrown into battle, horse racing reappeared, with the Ninth's commander and Michael both taking part. An April 12, 1863, entry in a diary kept by Corporal Timothy J. Regan of the Ninth mentions that both men had horses that ran in a competition. Regan wrote: "This afternoon we had a horse race which was taken part in by nags owned by General Griffin, Colonel Guiney, Lieutenant Colonel Hanly [sic] Adjutant Phalon [sic], Colonel Sweitzer, and General Sykes."[23]

Guiney was caught up in horse racing. A letter from him to his wife dated Sept. 11, 1863, described his love of it. "Horse-racing is all the talk and trouble and excitement now," he wrote. "The rebels just across the river are no account compared to—horses. I ran my black against the hitherto victorious horse 'Dick' of Lt. Col. Hanley. Mine won, in fact, shot right by his opponent. Tomorrow my horse runs again and I am going to keep him on the track until he beats everything in the Army or is clearly beaten himself."

In that same correspondence the colonel notes that "Flynn + Dr. Sullivan [surgeon James F. Sullivan], Phalen and myself are all well."[24]

Moments of wartime levity would be shattered for Guiney with the Battle of the Wilderness in May of 1864, when he was shot in the head and ended up losing his left eye. He returned home to his wife and daughter in Roxbury, Massachusetts.[25]

One can imagine the sorrow that Michael would have felt at his commander's—and friend's—situation. He and the men of the Ninth would fight on until the regiment's three-year enlistment ended June 10, 1864. Boarding a train in Washington and back in Boston by June 15th, the men would be greeted by thousands of friends and relatives and by a still-recuperating Guiney, noted Macnamara. The regiment was mustered out of the service June 21, 1864.[26]

Macnamara later wrote of Guiney: "In civil life, after the war, in the city of Boston, his reputation and abilities brought him prominently before the public, more particularly as assistant district attorney of the superior court, and later, when elected to the office of register of probate, etc., of Suffolk County."[27] Macnamara's book became a valuable resource for writers, including Frank J. Flynn, who encapsulated much of its commentary in "'The Fighting Ninth' for Fifty Years' and the Semi-Centennial Celebration," a 1911 tribute to the fiftieth anniversary of the Ninth Massachusetts' mustering-in. Macnamara's brother James, who died at the Battle of the Wilderness, had written a diary of his war experiences, and brother Michael wrote a book titled "The Irish Ninth in Bivouac and Battle."[28]

chapter XI

A HOMECOMING: STARTING OVER

Michael William Phalen was awarded various medals during his service in the Civil War and afterward as a member of patriotic organizations such as the Military Order of the Loyal Legion of the United States and the Grand Army of the Republic. The medals were kept in a glass-encased box by William "Bill" Phalen's family. Photo by Ashli Truchon.

Commonwealth of Massachusetts

CITY OF SALEM

CERTIFICATE OF MARRIAGE

GROOM	BRIDE
Name MICHAEL W. PHALEN	Name MARGARET RYAN
Surname After Marriage ----	Surname After Marriage ----
Residence SALEM, MASS.	Residence SALEM, MASS.
Age/DOB 22 Color WHITE	Age/DOB 20 Color WHITE
Occupation CURRIER	Occupation ----
Birthplace SALEM, MASS.	Birthplace IRELAND
Father's Name LAWRENCE PHALEN	Father's Name PATRICK RYAN
Mother's maiden Name ANNA -----	Mother's maiden Name HONORA -----
No. of Marriage 2ND	No. of Marriage 1ST
Date of Marriage AUGUST 22, 1864	Place of Marriage SALEM, MASS.
Person By whom married THOMAS H. SHANAN, CLERGY OF SALEM	
Date of Record AUGUST 25, 1864	

VOL. 10, PAGE 67, CERT. NO. 162

In 1864, shortly after his Civil War duty was over, Michael William Phalen married his second wife, Margaret "Maggie" Ryan, in Salem, Massachusetts. The marriage certificate notes that she was born in Ireland but mistakenly says he was born in Massachusetts, not Nova Scotia.

XI

Before the conflict would end, Michael fought with the Ninth Regiment in companies D, E, I and F and as Adjutant. He was mustered out of the army June 21, 1864, and lived for a time at the same address as mother Ann Phalen, in Salem, Massachusetts.[1] One can imagine her relief at having him home safely. Surely, there would have been celebrating then and when he married Margaret "Maggie" Ryan, a dressmaker and native of Ireland, a short time later, on August 22, 1864.[2]

If Michael had not already moved away from Massachusetts by October 1864, he would have been able to meet with his brother Edward, who was in Boston on temporary recruitment duty. There may have been time for them to enjoy family gatherings, and for each to share with the other stories of the horrors of war, of the brave men they knew and sometimes lost, and their plans for the future. Edward would rejoin his comrades in the 2nd Regiment Massachusetts Volunteer Infantry on the fields of battle, and would not leave the service until the Civil War was over in 1865. He, too, would come back to mom Ann's home.

Michael, a currier when he married his second wife, would be living in Chicago sometime in 1864, according to a government form he filled out decades later. It is known that he was in Chicago at least by 1866 and a partner in a business by 1867, according to other information.[3] The resiliency he displayed during the war would be called upon during the personal trials he would face as a husband and father, and in the world of business.

LOOKING BACK ON WAR: A CITIZEN IN SPIRIT AND DEED

A July 17, 1862, law passed by Congress allowed aliens 21 years of age and older who had lived in the country for a year, volunteered for military service and been honorably discharged to become United States citizens, if they sought it.[4] Michael, however, did not undergo naturalization until October 22, 1894, when he was 52 years old.[5] Perhaps he felt as if he already was an American and did not need to go through a formality; maybe he did not have time to think of it in a life that was full of challenges; perhaps he could not foresee the political and economic gains Irish-Americans might receive one day in being able to vote in a bloc; or maybe the value of citizenship was still an evolving notion for some during that time.

Scholars have pointed to the Civil War as a watershed in the concept of citizenship in the United States. Christian G. Samito has written:

"The modern American vision of national citizenship began to develop as a result of the tumult of the Civil War. Events leading up to and occurring during the 1860s challenged Americans to think about national citizenship in definite terms for the first time and the concept emerged dramatically transformed. During the 1860s, a distinctly American citizenship crystallized into a form that eventually integrated national rights and duties along with notions of loyalty and the embrace of American ideals."[6]

Citizenship or not, it seems undeniable that Michael was a loyal patriot and held an unwavering commitment to a strong United States; this is evidenced in his service during the Civil War and, afterward, in the company he would keep as a member of the Military Order of the Loyal Legion of the United States (MOLLUS). The organization, which came about after Lincoln's assassination, drew military officers and veteran Civil War officers who wanted to prevent future threats to the national government; it attracted the likes of Gen. Ulysses S. Grant, Major Gen. George Armstrong Custer and a stream of other notables, including, like Grant, other veterans who became U.S. presidents.[7]

Michael, who would move to Chicago after the Civil War, also was a member of the Grand Army of the Republic (GAR), a fraternal group of former Union military men who served in the Civil War. Founded in about 1866 in Illinois, GAR became a national organization with many local entities. His Chicago group was the George H. Thomas Post No. 5, Department of Illinois.[8] An old history of the post indicates that members had uniforms made and wore them during Chicago's 1877 railroad riots, from July 23rd to the 30th, and "with rifle in hand and ammunition in pouch, helped to keep order in the city."[9] Perhaps Michael played such a role. His great-grandson, Bill Phalen, remembers his family speaking of the man in the old photo, Michael, as "the captain." Perhaps that designation came from a rank he picked up in the GAR, or through his membership in the Western Society of the Army of the Potomac. With a neat hand and efficiency proven in war and in business, he was the latter organization's secretary in 1906.[10]

chapter XII

A New Horizon: Chicago

The historic Great Chicago Fire, October 8-10, 1871, sent shooting flames across the city, destroying much in its path and wreaking havoc with the lives of Bill Phalen's ancestors. In this 1871 stereo photo by Melander & Henderson, men survey the destruction at the corner of LaSalle and Washington streets. Photo courtesy of the Library of Congress.

An 1870 map shows Chicago's growth, radiating out from Lake Michigan.

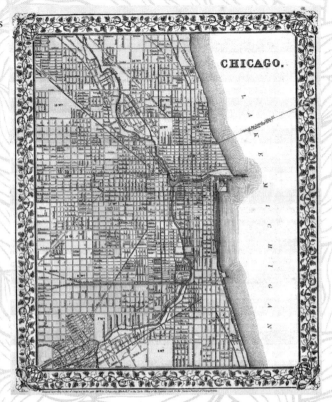

The Great Chicago Fire made a ruin of a large post office building, seen in this 1871 stereo photo by P.B. Greene. Photo courtesy of the Library of Congress.

XII

ot long after being honorably discharged from the Union Army, Michael left New England with new wife Margaret to set up home in Chicago, open his own business and start a family.[1]

If being among people of Irish Catholic descent in a strange new place was important to the young Phalens, they would not be disappointed. The Irish had been in Chicago since the city's early days, in the 1830s, and many more arrived from the 1840s on as refugees of Ireland's Great Famine. One estimate has it that by 1850, Irish immigrants made up approximately a fifth of the city's population.[2]

Michael likely had heard of good prospects that awaited in the rapidly growing city. During the Civil War, Chicago-area companies had been selling horses, hardtack, preserved meat, tents, harnesses, saddles and other wares to the Union Army for the troops; the city's heavy industry provided Union forces with the rolling stock and rails necessary to transport the troops and supplies. The Union Stock Yard, which opened in 1865, became a center for meatpacking.[3] Hides would have been a natural spinoff of that industry, and Michael, with experience as a tanner, apparently took advantage of that fact to open his own business.[4]

Opportunities in their new locale would not spare him and his wife personal tragedy, however. A son, Edward S. Phalen, died in November 1870 at the age of three years, eleven months and three days; he was buried Nov. 15, 1870, the same day as his four-day-old sister Emma; they likely had died of the same contagion. A daughter, Amy, born in 1869, died at eleven months and seven days on August 2, 1870. A son born January 27, 1872, also named Edward, died in May of 1872 at the age of five months. In the midst of what must have seemed like hopelessness and dread, his twin brother, William Joseph, happily survived to live a long life and eventually become the grandfather of today's Bill Phalen.[5]

That the Phalen children died so young was horrible but, sadly, not unusual. It has been estimated that 20 to 35 percent of all those born in late-19th-century cities died within a year. With antibiotics yet to be discovered, causes of deaths among children included communicable childhood diseases, diarrheal diseases and gastroenteritis, and pneumonia and other respiratory ailments, which in later times might easily have been cured.[6]

The Phalen children who succumbed to illnesses were buried at Calvary Catholic Cemetery in Evanston, Illinois, on the outskirts of Chicago. Michael had purchased a family plot there on August, 26, 1868, as a final resting place for a baby named Mary Agnes Sullivan; she was interred there eleven days later at twenty months of age.[7] It is not known what relationship Michael had with baby Sullivan's mother: Was she the widow of an army friend? There were many Sullivans in the Ninth Regiment. Was she a friend of both Margaret and Michael, a woman who had fallen on hard times? Or had Michael and the baby's mother been in a romantic relationship? The story is lost to history.

In Chicago after the Civil War, Michael is described as dealing in hides and leather. His occupation is similarly noted in the 1870 U.S. Census, where he was described as a hide-and-leather dealer who owned $3,700 worth of real estate and had $4,500 worth of personal property.[8] He may have been prospering, but he, along with his wife, would have been dealing with profound grief. This was the year in which they had lost their three little ones. The next year, 1871, Margaret became pregnant with the twins. If that pregnancy was a time of hope for the couple, there instead would be more anguish. Michael's business was wiped out by the Great Chicago Fire, October 8-10, 1871.[9] Margaret was then in the last few months of her pregnancy.

In a city with many wooden structures and even sidewalks of wood, "Chicago had had a number of big fires, but this was a fire like no one had ever even heard of," writes historian Donald L. Miller.

"The flames seemed to be shooting from a massive blowtorch somewhere off in the sky. The heat was so intense it melted iron and steel (which melt, respectively, at two-thousand degrees and twenty-five hundred degrees Fahrenheit), turned stone to powder and marble and granite to lime, and made trees explode from the heat of their own resin. People running from the fire could feel its heat through their backs, burning their lungs."[10]

Author William Cronon writes: "Terrified inhabitants fled amid scenes of gothic horror: parents searching for lost children, looters picking through abandoned buildings, mobs crowding collapsing bridges, whole city blocks engulfed in flames."[11] Michael and a pregnant Margaret may have endured such bedlam and destruction or at least been witness to it.

In addition to the loss of property and seventy-three miles of streets and 17,450 buildings, almost 100,000 people were left homeless after the Chicago fire, states Miller.[12] No evidence has been discovered to suggest that Michael and his wife were homeless, but with no business to fall back on in a fire-devastated city, they must have been eating any savings they might have had. Eight months later, still in Chicago, they would lose twin Edward.

Sometime after the infant's death, Michael, wife Margaret and surviving baby William Joseph moved back to Massachusetts, where they had family.[13] One can imagine Michael's mother, Ann Phalen, welcoming them and offering solace for their heavy losses, the worst, the loss of a baby. This mother and grandmother surely would have treasured her time with little grandson William Joseph, whom she may never have met. Michael would be able to see his sisters and brother Edward. He may have been pained by what must have been a noticeable degeneration of Edward's war-wounded arm. With no time to waste and a family to support, entrepreneurial Michael would endeavor to start over in the same leather-related business that was burned out in Chicago, only to lose it in the Great Boston Fire, November 9-10, 1872.[14]

By early the next year, the Phalens were back in Chicago.[15] Historians have long observed that the city rebounded remarkably, if not miraculously, well after the Great Chicago Fire. Perhaps Michael saw that there was more opportunity to be found in Chicago than in burned-out Boston. Writes Cronon of Chicago's fire: "The fire may have destroyed the downtown, but it left Chicago's essential infrastructure intact: most of the grain elevators still stood, and the lumber district, stockyards and factories were well outside the burn." The metaphorical image that appeared for the next quarter century, he observes, was "the city as phoenix," the magical bird that could find rebirth in ashes.[16]

In what a modern-day relative-turned-researcher described as Margaret's and Michael's "star-crossed marriage," it would not be long before disaster again struck. After a four-month battle for her life, Margaret Phalen died in 1873 of consumption.[17] She died March 3, 1873, and was interred at Calvary Catholic Cemetery.[18] She left behind baby William Joseph, little more than thirteen months old, and her husband, Michael.

Michael, who had lost one wife when he was fighting in the Civil War, and now another, was a man with a baby to take care of; and, apparently with the same strength and determination he had shown on a battlefield—when he was injured yet continued to fight—he moved on with his life. Did he leave little William Joseph in the care of a friend or a babysitter as he worked in Chicago, or might he have taken the baby back to family in Massachusetts for a time? The answers lie behind the veil of history.

chapter XIII

Moving On With Life

In this circa 1905 photo taken at Chicago's Lincoln Park, Lake Shore Drive came very close to the edge of Lake Michigan, and horse-driven contrivances were the mode of travel. Library of Congress, Prints & Photographs Division, Detroit Publishing Co. Collection, LC-D4-10865.

XIII

After experiencing multiple tragedies and disasters, Michael would be tested again after he married his third wife, Mary H. Curtin, in 1874.[1] Two of their children, Sidney and Helen, died, respectively, at twelve months in July of 1878, and at eleven days old in June of 1881. They were interred with Michael's other little ones at Calvary Catholic Cemetery.[2] Sons Frank and Charles Phalen survived, however, and they and William Joseph were raised as brothers as the family moved to various Chicago settings. Michael, during this period, was successful and gained experience in a variety of endeavors, including the steel business.

Information about Michael from 1866 on, including where he and his wife and children lived and his places of employment, as well as family marriages and births of children, was pieced together based on notations family members found in old city directories, in military pension records and from other sources.[3] Details follow:

• The Edwards' Chicago Directory of 1866 has Michael living at 134 Coolidge.

• In 1867, both the Edwards' Chicago Directory and Baileys [sic] Directory list him under Hides and Leathers as M.W. Phalon [sic] at 163 Kinzie Street. The same year he is listed as a partner of W.H. Mooney and Company, and was living at 215 Park Avenue.

• The U.S. Census [Illinois] for 1870 lists him as a hides and leather dealer, age 27.

• In Merchant's Chicago Census Report of 1871 and Edwards' Chicago Directory of that year, he is listed as a leather dealer at 115 Kinzie Street, and living at 214 Sampson.

• The Edwards' Chicago Directory of 1873 [the year his wife Margaret died] reported Michael boarding at the Central Hotel at Madison and Washington.

- The 1874-'75 Lakeside Directory, Vol. II, saw him working at Beach and Hale Company, and boarding at the DeForest Home.
- The 1876-'77 Lakeside Directory noted that he was a bookkeeper at 22 South Jefferson, and still boarding at the DeForest Home.
- The 1877-'78 Lakeside Directory showed him working at 22 South Jefferson, and living at a different location, 42 Honore Street.
- The 1880 Lakeside Directory noted that he was working as a traveling agent at 163 Lake Street.
- The 1881 Lakeside Directory reported that he still was a traveling agent at 163 Lake Street, and living elsewhere, at 67 Rush Street.
- From about 1882: He was national chairman of the Traveler's Protective Association railway committee during his time as a traveling salesman. The nonprofit organization, described as a type of insurance firm for this industry, was founded in 1882 in Chicago with the objective of providing its members special concessions from hotels, railroads and other transportation agencies, and to handle grievances of members.
- The 1883 Lakeside Directory noted that he was affiliated with a firm in which he appears to have been a partner, named Gurney and Phalen at 249 Lake Street; he was living at 67 Rush Street.
- The 1884 Lakeside Directory reported his occupation as a "commercial traveler" at 247 Lake Street, and his residence as 10 Scott Street. He had by now separated from his former business association and appears to have formed a new business, Phalen and McNurtney.
- In 1885, Michael changes employment and works for Chas. H. Gurney and Company at 249 Lake Street; he was still living at 10 Scott Street.
- In 1886, the Lakeside Directory reported him working at Northwestern Screw Company at Loomis and Tayler [sic], and residing at 10 Scott Street.
- In 1887-'88, he is cited as M. William Phalen, and has returned to Chas. H. Gurney and Company as a salesman; he is still living at 10 Scott Street.
- By 1889, Michael has been promoted to manager of Chas. H. Gurney and Company and has moved his family to 397 State Street.
- In 1890-'91, Michael was climbing the business ladder once again and is listed as secretary of Chas. H. Gurney and Company; he remains with his family at the State Street location. Son William Joseph Phalen, still

living at home, now works as a buyer for C.H. Gurney and Company. Son Frank joins the company as a clerk in 1892.

In 1895, the family moves to 49 Astor Street. William Joseph (Bill Phalen's grandfather) marries Margaret Mullen Schieble (Bill's grandmother) this same year at Chicago's Holy Name Cathedral; half brother Frank was best man. The newlyweds take up residence at 16 Burton Place. Michael's son Frank is promoted to city buyer at C.H. Gurney and Company.

• In 1896, William Joseph Phalen and wife Margaret have a son (named Robert, after his maternal grandfather, Robert Chambers).

• In 1897, Michael was employed as the Chicago representative of the Atha and Illingworth Steel Company (it became Crucible Steel Company); the U.S. Navy Department had engaged Atha and Illingworth to make steel gun forgings for ships. Michael and his wife moved to 1580 Kenmore Avenue [based on military pension records]. Also in 1897, twin sons, Richard Charles Chambers Phalen and Ralph John Laurence Phalen, are born to Bill Phalen's grandfather and grandmother, William Joseph and Margaret Phalen, who then lived at 22 Wisconsin Avenue. Richard would grow up to marry Lucille Pritchard in 1934. They were Bill Phalen's parents.

• In 1898, Michael is working as a manager at 10 South Canal Street. Son William Joseph Phalen, meanwhile, has moved his family to 515 Evanston Avenue and the following year to 1843 Aldine Avenue, where William Joseph Phalen II is born.

• At the turn of the twentieth century, Michael is still a manager at 10 South Canal Street, and his son Frank is employed there as a salesman. William Joseph Phalen (Bill Phalen's grandfather), is working as a superintendent at a firm located at 1624 Belmont Avenue. Michael and his wife lived at 1580 Kenmore Avenue for the rest of their thirty-four-year marriage.

chapter XIV

A New 'War' - A Bureaucratic Skirmish

After the Civil War, Michael William Phalen became a businessman in Chicago, where he also was a member of national patriotic organizations, such as the Military Order of the Loyal Legion of the United States (MOLLUS). Photo courtesy of Mass. Commandery MOLLUS/U.S. Army Heritage and Education Center, Carlisle, Pennsylvania.

Yours Truly,

M W Phalen

1580 Kenmore Ave

Chicago

As a Civil War adjutant, serving on various battlefields, Michael William Phalen would have affixed his precise signature to numerous official reports. In later years, he would be facing a civilian battle and writing letters to an often-bureaucratic government pension board.

XIV

Michael began experiencing physical ailments at around age fifty. He at first attributed them to rheumatism and urinary issues, and later, as his health declined, to intestinal problems and heart disease.

Enlisting the services of a Chicago law firm specializing in pensions, Milo B. Stevens & Co., Michael in 1892 applied for a health-related military pension governed by a federal statute (the Act of June 27, 1890).[1] The law permitted veterans of the Civil War ("War of the Rebellion"), who had served for ninety days or more and were honorably discharged, to qualify for an invalid pension according to certain standards: in short, whether and to what degree their ailments, including mental or physical, rendered them incapacitated for manual labor. It was up to pension-board medical examiners to diagnose health issues and ascertain whether those conditions would prevent a veteran from performing manual work. Pension rates ranged from six dollars to twelve dollars a month.[2]

Michael's original pension "declaration," or application (April 7, 1892), signed by him but possibly filled out by his lawyer, specified his age as forty-nine instead of the fifty he would have been if born in 1842. The age discrepancy apparently continued unquestioned through all of Michael's dealings with the Department of Interior Bureau of Pensions over the fifteen years in which his health steadily worsened.[3]

The Bureau of Pensions, possibly beleaguered by an onslaught of claims with the new law, moved at the proverbial snail's pace. For example, Michael's initial pension application, stamped as having reached the Pension Office on April 13, 1892, was first considered May 31 of that year and came back to Michael requesting more information about a war injury; records show that Michael, filling in blanks, had included "wound of forehead" on his original pension application in a space that called for all diseases, wounds and injuries. Furnishing more information, he provided a notarized affidavit as follows: "That in answer to the Pension Office call of June 1, 1892, I have to state that wound of forehead was received on June 27, 1862, in the battle of Gaines Mill, Va., received while in action with the enemy."[4]

The question of whether he was entitled to the pension dragged on in bureaucratic fashion. More than a year later, on August 10, 1893, the Bureau of Pensions was asking the War Department's Record and Pension Office "to furnish a report with the full military and medical history of the soldier." An Army colonel wrote that Michael's medical records show him as follows: "As M.W. Phelan [sic], Lieut., Co. D, 9 Mass. Vols., wounded slightly at the battle of Mechanicsville, Gaines Mills Va. & Malvern, Va., June 27, 62, Nothing additional found."[5]

It might appear from this record that Michael also was hurt in some way shortly before and after the officially noted Gaines' Mill wound to his forehead. That would further account for the gallantry a compatriot in later years attributed to Michael in the Battle of Malvern Hill.

If one thing rings true from reading between all the lines of military records, Michael W. Phalen, the man who carried on in wartime with his own assessment of "merely a scratch," was no crybaby.

The applications he filed in 1892, 1899 and 1900 did not yield any pension funds.[6] While no medical reports were found to coincide with the first two filings, an existing 1900 medical report showed that Michael, noted as age 57 (that would put his birth year at 1843), and a salesman with soft palms, no longer complained of urinary problems; he felt discomfort from what he believed to be rheumatism in his left shoulder and side, and also indigestion. He told the examiners that he was not bothered by the old Civil War wound to his head.

The handwritten medical report noted the wound's remnant and its lack of physical effects on the patient: "At margin of hair in center of forehead is a small superficial scar - not tender, dragging or adherent. No depression of bone. No evidence of diseased condition of brain or membranes. No vertigo, spasms, convulsions or nausea. No local or general [term not clear; possibly paralysis]. No hemiplegia or paraplegia. Mental condition sound." His heart was "normal in size, position, sounds, force and rhythm. No murmurs. No dyspnoea, oedema, cyanosis." Aside from being diagnosed as having some sore lumbar region muscles, Michael was given a clean bill of health. At the time, he was five feet, ten and a half inches tall and weighed two hundred twenty-six pounds.[7] (See *Addendum: Medical*, for full report.)

In 1905, Michael, by then retired (he listed "none" at the pension form's occupation category), was granted a partial invalid pension; despite a surgeon's suggestion that he receive eight dollars a month, the medical board approved a six-dollar-a-month pension, noting rheumatism (Michael's original complaint), deafness in one ear, senile debility and "stomach trouble" as causative factors. As pertaining to the latter, Michael said during the medical examination that he had been suffering intestinal trouble for five years and had lost twenty-five pounds within three months.

The examination concluded that his lungs and heart were normal. For whatever reason, possibly because the examiners noted his heart was normal during the exam, he "disclaimed" *disease of the heart*, as had been written on his complaint. By this time, he was slow of gait, his eyes were described as murky, his tongue brown-coated, his teeth in bad condition and his breath as having a foul odor. His stomach and colon were distended with gas, and his stomach was tender to the touch.

With dark-gray hair, a dark complexion and hazel eyes, Michael stood five feet, ten inches tall and weighed two hundred pounds. His age was written as sixty-two (that would have put his birth year at 1843 instead of the church record's 1842). The medical report noted that he appeared to be sixty-eight years old.[8] (See *Addendum: Medical*, for full report.)

The following year, in September of 1906, Michael's attorney applied for reconsideration of a pension increase, citing his client's chronic dyspepsia, rheumatism, failing sight, deafness and, again, "disease of heart" as reasons. This time around, Michael did not "disclaim" heart issues and told medical examiners that he had been experiencing heart problems for three years. There is no evidence that he received a pension increase or had another pension-board-ordered medical examination that year.[9]

A 1907 medical report listed Michael's age as sixty-three (that would have put his year of birth at 1844). Whether Michael produced a personal physician's diagnosis as proof of heart disease for the pension board during the physical examination on January 2, 1907, is unknown. What is a matter of record is that pension board medical examiners cited rheumatism and disease of stomach as reasons enough for a pension increase, but not heart disease. Their conclusion, in strictly layman's terms, was that Michael's heart was not enlarged, and he was not experiencing heart-related symptoms such as breathing difficulties, bluish skin associated with lack of oxygenation, and fluid retention: The record notes, "heart, apex in the normal position, no hypertrophy or dilitation, no cyanosis, dyspnea or oedema."

The pension was allowed to increase to eight dollars a month on the basis of Michael's rheumatism, "disease of the stomach" and also senile debility. (The medical examiner had suggested that a ten-dollar-a-month pension was warranted).[10] (See *Addendum: Medical*, for full report).

After all the back-and-forth dealings with the Pension Bureau over 15 years, a federal law (Act of February 6, 1907), enacted about a month after Michael's January medical exam, rendered the raise a moot point; the new ruling entitled him to a twelve-dollar-a-month pension. The act did not require a veteran to have a disability. The raise went to persons who had served ninety days or more in the U.S. military during the Civil War or sixty days in the war with Mexico; the pension amount rose depending on age, with those who had reached age sixty-two receiving twelve dollars per month; those reaching seventy years got fifteen dollars per month; and at seventy-five years or older, pensioners received twenty dollars a month.[11] Michael was of the right age to qualify for the lower end of this pension's raise; but quite ill, he would not live much longer to appreciate his quasi-victory.

He died March 14, 1908. A story passed down by family relates that his heart may have given out after he was shoveling snow. A Chicago Department of Health vital statistics report, likely based on a doctor's diagnosis, does cite the cause of his demise as heart failure due to overexertion, along with a two-year duration of endocarditis, and also gastritis.[12] Perhaps in 1907 the Bureau of Pensions medical examiners did not have a way to test Michael for possibly serious heart-related symptoms related to endocarditis.

The report of Michael's death estimated that he died at age sixty-four, but based on records from Halifax, Nova Scotia, where Michael was born, the date of his birth was eight days before his September 4, 1842, baptism at St. Mary's Basilica in Halifax.[13] That would put his age at the time of his death at sixty-six.

Michael himself might point out that even he had made a mistake or two in the volumes of paperwork required to request pension increases; in a neat and polite handwritten note that looks as if it were penned today, he sought to correct any misunderstanding that might have reached the Bureau of Pensions.[14] He wrote, as follows:

Chicago Aug. 3. 1905
The Commissioner of Pensions
Washington, D.C.
Dear Sir: I return herewith form 3-447 filled out as requested but I
made several errors and afterward mislaid form 3-389. If you will kindly
forward another form I will fill it out and return it.
Yours truly
MW Phalen
1580 Kenmore Ave
Chicago

As it turns out, form 3-447 was a thirteen-question survey Michael had received from the Department of the Interior, Bureau of Pensions, and mailed back July 20, 1905. The purpose of the request for information ostensibly was to prevent "any one falsely personating [sic] you, or otherwise committing fraud in your name . . ."[15] It may be that an error Michael discovered was how he had filled out when he was born. He had written Sept. 4, 1843 (a year later than his baptism date).

Paperwork. Form numbers. Putting up with a bit of a bureaucratic quagmire in his later years seems minor compared with what Michael endured in his lifetime: Fighting in the Civil War to save a nation from collapse; losing children and wives to illnesses; losing businesses to two epic fires; embarking on building a new family and losing more infants; and rebuilding a career. Taken together, these seem elements of some grand novel or a richly themed play. But for this man—loved by three women, admired and liked by his peers during and after the war, and no stranger to tragedy—his drama was the theater of real life.

While he had to live through rough spots, Michael likely would agree that he also had lived in pretty exhilarating times for Americans—in fact, the stuff of which history books are made. He was on hand for the infancy of the telephone, electric power, the automobile and the dawn of flight, to name a few important advances. Alexander Graham Bell obtained a patent for the telephone in 1876; Thomas Alva Edison, who had provided some scientific contribution to the development of the telephone, patented the incandescent light bulb in 1883, ultimately leading to the lighting up of U.S. cities, and more.[16]

Likely having grown up with oil lamps for lighting, and later gas lamps[17], Michael was about to see big changes beginning in 1888. That is when the Chicago Edison Company opened an electric station with a capacity to power 10,000 lights in the offices of the financial district around Adams and LaSalle streets. One cannot imagine that Michael would not have been among the crowds at Chicago's 1893 World's Columbian Exposition. According to a report in the *Encyclopedia of Chicago*, "Henry Ford saw an internal combustion engine at the fair that fired his dreams about the possibility of designing a horseless carriage. For millions of visitors, the electrical illuminations of the fair were a source of wonder and excitement about the possibilities of illuminating America's farms and cities." Michael already would have observed State Street's horsecars replaced by cable cars in 1882; he would see these contrivances yielding to electric trolleys in 1906.[18]

A few matters of history: Henry Ford did build an experimental gasoline-powered motor car—the Quadricycle—in 1896; he founded Ford Motor Company in 1903, the same year that the Wright brothers—Orville and Wilbur—made the first successful airplane flights. Ford's iconic Model T Ford, or Tin Lizzie, came out in 1908, the October after Michael's death. The first mass-produced automobile, made on assembly lines, was relatively affordable and revolutionized the way people would get about. Chances are that Michael, the guy who had raced horses in the midst of the Civil War, would have loved driving an automobile up and down Michigan Avenue!

chapter XV

EDWARD AUGUSTUS PHALEN

Edward Augustus Phalen, brother of Michael William Phalen, served with the 2nd Regiment Massachusetts Volunteer Infantry during the U.S. Civil War. Photo courtesy of Mass. Commandery MOLLUS/U.S. Army Heritage and Education Center, Carlisle, Pennsylvania. Photo correction by Frank Fernandez.

With an artistic flourish, Edward's signature was reflective of a long-ago era.

XV

I t is unusual enough for one to learn of the existence of a single Civil War ancestor. Bill Phalen came up a winner in his genealogical tryst. As noted, he found out he had a second brave relative who served the country in that time of crisis—his great-grandfather's brother Edward. His story, often sad, deserves to be told—as an acknowledgment of his place in the fabric of American history.

Edward Augustus Phalen was a shoemaker when he enlisted at age 21 on May 25, 1861, to serve in Company C of the 2nd Regiment Massachusetts Volunteer Infantry.[1] He served with his regiment during the full four years of the Civil War, suffering wounds and contracting malaria along the way, and earning rapid promotions.[2] After attaining the rank of first sergeant October 12, 1861, he was commissioned second lieutenant, July 13, 1862; first lieutenant, November 9, 1862; and captain, March 31, 1863.[3]

Trained on West Roxbury farmland dubbed Camp Andrew (after then-Massachusetts Governor John Albion Andrew), the 2nd Regiment Massachusetts Volunteer Infantry left Boston by train on July 8, 1861. In a memoir of his Civil War service, a gentleman named Henry Newton Comey, a former captain in Edward's regiment, recalled the crowds that had assembled to see their loved ones off. "Thousands had gathered to wave flags and cheer us on," recollected Comey, who, like Edward, had entered the army as a private. Perhaps Edward's mom and other family members, too, were among the throng, giving him last-minute embraces and encouragement.

Patriotic fervor was lavished on the 1,040-strong regiment the next morning as well in New York City, according to Comey; the troops had reached there overnight by way of a steamboat picked up at Groton, Connecticut, he noted. As a surprise, the entire regiment was treated to breakfast at New York's "beautiful" Astor Hotel. "It was obvious that the owner was a staunch patriot and this was his way of contributing to the support of the Union," penned Comey. "Although we ate in shifts, the hotel staff were very good natured and there seemed to be no limit to the eggs, bacon, ham, steaks and coffee for this hungry army."

Later, on board a train traveling through New Jersey and Pennsylvania, Comey observed lovely scenery—the same rivers and fields of wheat and corn that Edward would have seen, and there were more shows of affectionate patriotism from cheering citizens. "In many places a drink and victuals were brought to us by the ladies of the area," remembered Comey. "We were awakened near the Pennsylvania-Maryland Line by several ladies with more collations, including pies and cakes. They crowded around the railroad cars to shake our hands and bid us 'God Speed.'" Those peaceful moments were soon to end, with four years of war ahead.

Comey wrote: "We arrived at Hagerstown, Maryland, at about 7 a.m., and were greeted at the station by Union Army sentinels. It was now obvious that we had left the friendly areas and the fields of battle would not be very far."[4]

chapter XVI

INTO THE FRAY

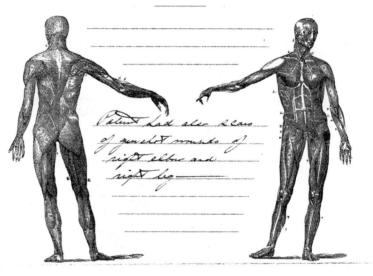

LOCATION OF INJURIES.

Patient had also 2 scars of gunshot wounds of right elbow and right leg

I further declare that I have no interest in said case, and am not concerned in its prosecution, and am not related to the claimant.

P. O. Address,

Civil War wounds to Edward Augustus Phalen's right elbow and right leg are noted in a physician's medical record, on which body parts are illustrated in distinctive 19th-century detail.

Edward Augustus Phalen was a captain in the 2nd Regiment Massachusetts Volunteer Infantry during the Civil War. This monument at the Gettysburg Battlefield honors the men of his unit, who served with valor there. Photo courtesy of the National Park Service.

XVI

The 2nd Regiment Massachusetts Volunteer Infantry ultimately went on to serve in several major Civil War campaigns, including historic Antietam and Gettysburg, and also General William Tecumseh Sherman's famed Atlanta Campaign (May 1-September 1864) and March to the Sea (September-December, 1864). From the burning of Atlanta, depicted in the 1939 movie "Gone With the Wind," to the march to the Atlantic Coast, just below Savannah, Georgia, the troops scored Union victories by "decimating Confederate supply lines and property along the way."[1]

Edward had been wounded in his right forearm and right thigh during the Battle of Cedar Mountain, August 9, 1862, in Culpeper County, Virginia.[2] The injury to his arm would cause him problems the rest of his life.

The Battle of Cedar Mountain was a victory for the Confederate Army, which reportedly outnumbered Union soldiers two to one.[3] Even the weather—brutally hot—was a formidable foe that day. In his memoir, Comey said a new recruit had died from heat exhaustion and was buried by the roadside. "This was going to be one of the hottest days of the summer, at least 100 degrees, with high humidity. The clouds of dust were so thick we could not even see the column in our front. We were all choking and rubbing our eyes," he recalled.[4]

Commander of the Army of Virginia Major General John Pope, in an official report, noted the torrid weather during the Saturday battle: "The fatigue of the troops, from long marches and excessive heat, made it impossible for either side to resume the action on Sunday. ... Monday was spent in burying the dead and getting off the wounded. The slaughter was severe on both sides, most of the fighting being hand to hand. The dead bodies of both armies were found mingled together in masses over the whole ground of the conflict. The burying of the dead was not completed until dark on Monday, the heat being so terrible that severe work was not possible."[5]

The battle's wounded were moved to the town of Culpeper, where houses, churches, shops and a hotel were being used as hospitals.[6] Edward, one of ninety-three wounded men, might have been taken to one of those makeshift facilities before being transported by ambulance wagon to a medical facility in Alexandria, Virginia.[7] Army records show that after Edward was shot he spent time at Alexandria's Wolfe Street Hospital.[8] Formerly used by the public, it became a hospital for Union troops during the war.[9] Nine days after he was shot, a newspaper article in the hometown *Salem Register* on August 18, 1862, noted: "Ist Sergt. E.A. Phalen" was wounded in the arm and leg in the Battle of Cedar Mountain.[10]

In what turned out to be a lengthy convalescence, Edward was later hospitalized during the months of September and October of 1862 in a facility located on Davids Island off New York City.[11]

Because of the large numbers of Civil War wounded, the War Department, in 1862, subleased Davids Island to create a U.S. Army hospital, De Camp General Hospital; it opened in May of that year. A *New York Times* article dated August 13, 1862, reported: "There are now about 900 sick and wounded soldiers at the hospitals on David's [sic] Island. Since their conveyance there a large number have died, but the great majority are doing well, and fast recovering."[12]

It would not be a fast recovery for Edward, however. Requiring sick leave at various times after his hospitalization due to his war wounds, he was still having medical problems into 1863, when he was captain of Company B. It is unclear as to whether fighting during the Battle of Gettysburg (July 1-3, 1863) had exacerbated Edward's old wound or there was a new injury to the same right arm. Whatever the case, a U.S. Army surgeon based in Boston, in a report dated July 27, 1863, noted that he had examined Edward and found him "unfit for duty" because of a gunshot wound of the right arm received at Gettysburg. Edward, he said, would "not be able to resume his duties in a less period than twenty days without incurring the risk of permanent disability."[13] Edward likely spent that leave in Salem, Massachusetts, recuperating among family members.

He would spend several months in Boston the following year when he was under special orders to recruit enlistees[14]; one might assume that Edward would have enjoyed the company of his mother and siblings, in nearby Salem, from time to time. Interestingly, Henry Newton Comey, in a postscript to a letter written to a sister on Oct. 18, 1864, from Atlanta stated: "P.S. Father will find Capt. Dennis Mehan and Edward Phalen in Scolleys Building, Boston. I need a watch very much. Would like to have you send that gold one out by Captain Mehan or Captain Phalen when they come out."[15] (Mehan in later years would testify as to Edward's bouts of malaria.)

Edward and Mehan returned to their regiment April 9, 1865, and Comey, by then a captain, received his own orders to perform recruitment duty in Massachusetts along with other captains.[16] He later wrote: "Meanwhile, the 2nd Mass. was consolidated, temporarily, into two companies, with Captain Phalen commanding." Comey, in his memoir, recounted the historically significant events that occurred during the next three weeks, including the death of Abraham Lincoln:

"When the army commenced marching again, on April 10th, we who were assigned to recruiting were on our way to a steamer which would take us to New York, to get to Massachusetts by rail. After limited success, we returned to our regiment on the 20th of May, 1865, with forty additional men. Many very important events had occurred since we left. General Lee surrendered to General Grant at Appomattox Court House, Virginia, on April 9th, and General Johnston and General Sherman signed an armistice agreement on the 18th. On the 14th came the terrible news of President Lincoln's assassination. The suspension of all hostilities was reported on April 20th, and the announcement of General Johnston's final surrender on the 29th. After that the 20th Corps had orders to March to Washington."[17]

Edward, part of that march, provided a historical record of sorts when he wrote a military report detailing his regiment's movement from Goldsborough, North Carolina, through Raleigh, North Carolina, from Richmond, Virginia, to Alexandria, Virginia, and then to end-of-war duty near and within Washington, D.C. An excerpt from the report of operations from April 10-May 19, 1865, which Capt. Edward A. Phalen provided for "Capt. J.R. Lindsay, Actg. Asst. Adjt. Gen., 2d Brig., 1st Div., 20th Army Corps," follows:

"On the 29th [of April] we received the announcement of the surrender of Johnston's army and orders to be in readiness to march the next morning for Washington via Richmond. Left Raleigh at 5 a.m. April 30, and arrived at or near Falling Creek, near Manchester, Va., five miles from Richmond May 9. Remained in camp at this place until the 11th, when we moved toward Alexandria.

We entered Richmond at 12 _m. and passed through the city in columns by companies. Encamped that night on Brook Creek, four miles from Richmond (north). Moved at 4.30 a.m. May 12, and arrived near Alexandria May 19, having made the march from Raleigh to Alexandria in twenty days.

I have the honor to be, very respectfully, your obedient servant, E.A. Phalen, Captain, Comdg. Second Massachusetts Veteran Vols."[18]

Edward was mustered out of the Union Army July 14, 1865, as captain of Company B.[19] He married Anna M. Sherwood June 17, 1869, and the couple had a son, William C. Phalen.[20] Somewhere along the way, Edward became a stenographer. But life did not proceed smoothly.

The illness and injuries that he had experienced on the battlefield saw him requesting an invalid, or disability, pension after the war, in 1867; a "ball" stayed forever lodged in his right thigh, but it was his wounded right arm and the effect it had on his hand that was the injury most troublesome to him, according to medical records.[21] War took a toll on his body as well as his ability to earn a living.

Edward would go through the formal process of requesting the U.S. Department of the Interior Bureau of Pensions for increases in his invalid pension, and submitting to the agency's required medical examinations throughout his years. A January, 14, 1867, report to the Bureau of Pensions by a Dr. David Choate noted that because of the wound to Edward's right arm the "rotation" of the hand was two-thirds of normal and that both the arm and right hand were weak. The "power to grasp, to lift, to do any work requiring much strength or quickness of movement [was] much reduced. Writing fatigues him. ... Another ball entered right thigh and remains in limb." Edward was granted his initial disability pay of seven dollars and fifty cents a month.[22]

With further weakness in his right hand by 1876, and then a problem with his right leg, he was entitled to fifteen dollars a month in invalid pay. By October 1889, as his health worsened, his disability pension rose to seventeen dollars a month.[23]

At least by 1890, Edward was also feeling the effects of the war-related malaria that had caused him problems decades earlier, and he sought a raise in his disability pay because of it. If the war was difficult for men like Edward to endure, receiving a raise to twenty-four dollars a month proved to be another battle.[24]

chapter XVII

A CALL FOR HELP

Officer's Certificate to Disability of Soldier.

_____ 186

I, *William Cogswell* do hereby certify that I was *Captain* of Company
C of the *Second* Regiment of *Massachusetts* Volunteers, and am
acquainted with *Edward A Phalen* who was a member of my Company, and, as I am
informed, is an applicant for an Invalid Pension. That the said *Edward A Phalen* was
Commissioned mustered into service on or about the *13th* day of *July* 1862 and discharged
At expiration of service about the *14th* day
of *July* 1865 having become disabled from doing duty as a soldier on or about
the *9th* day of *August* 1862 while in the service of the United
States, and in the line of his duty as a soldier, in the manner and at the place as follows :

*In battle of Cedar mountain Va. while 2d Lieut Co. F, and on duty with
Co. "C" he was wounded a his right arm and right leg, and sent to hospital
at Alexandria Va. for treatment His Commission was issued July 13 '62 but
by reason of the movements of the army he was unable to get mustered before the
battle and by reason of his wounds received thereupon unable to get mustered until
Oct 23d 1862 he was acting as 2d Lieut at the time he received his wounds and received
pay as such from the date of his commission*
My knowledge is derived from personal information

That the said soldier was in good health at the time he entered the service, and the disability above
referred to affected him while in the service and at his discharge, as follows : *Right arm useless,*
right leg lame and weak I am not interested in said soldier's claim for a pension

State of Massachusetts, County of *Essex* ss.
Salem Jany 30th 186 c Sworn to before me.
I am disinterested. I certify that deponent is
a credible person.

Wm Cogswell
Late Capt. Co C.
2 Regt. Mass. Inf

Geo H Choate J.P.

William Cogswell, once Edward Augustus Phalen's Civil War commander, went on
to serve in the U.S. Congress. In postwar affidavits to a government pension board,
he vouched for Edward's war wounds and a battlefield attack of malaria.

Examining Surgeon's Certificate.

Salem Mass Jan 14th, 1867

I hereby certify, That I have carefully examined
Edward A. Phalen Salem , late a 2d Lieut. in Company F of the
2d Regiment Mass Vols.

Applicant's service.

in the service of the United States, who was discharged at
Washington DC , on the 14th day of July ,
1865 , and is an applicant for an invalid pension, by reason of
alleged disability resulting from Gunshot wounds.

In my opinion the said Edward A. Phalen

Degree of disability.

is two thirds (2/3) incapacitated for obtaining his subsistence by
manual labor from the cause above stated.

Judging from his present condition, and from the evidence before

Origin.

me, it is my belief that the said disability was contracted
in the service aforesaid in the line of duty.

Probable duration.

The disability is probably for years.

A more particular description of the applicant's condition is
subjoined: Wounded Aug 9th 62. Right forearm & right thigh. Ball no 1. entered 3 inches below olecranon.

Particular description.

fracturing ulna, passing upward & inward & escaped from point just inside, internal condyle of humerus — hence
moderate atrophy of forearm. Motion of elbow joint free as to extent somewhat restricted as to ease & rapidity. Rotation
of hand about 2/3 the normal. Whole limb including hand, weak. Power to grasp to lift &to do any work, requiring much strength, or quickness of movement, much reduced. Writing fatigues. Some neuralgia in ends of
fingers. Ball no 2. entered right thigh, near knee: remains in limb. At present time, gives no serious
trouble.

David Choate M.D.

Examining Surgeon.

In 1867, a physician who had examined Edward Augustus Phalen advised the government pension board that gunshot wounds, in particular to Edward's right elbow and hand, would leave him disabled to a certain degree, "probably for years."

XVII

E dward and his family marshaled their "troops" for support. On September 4, 1890, Edward's Salem, Massachusetts, doctor, C.A. Carlson, provided information about Edward's condition for the Bureau of Pensions in an affidavit before a justice of the peace. Carlson told authorities that Edward had been in his care since 1876, during which time he had at various times attended him for malarial disease, including "some brain trouble with aphasia." He concluded: "I believe his disability is due to disease (malaria) contracted in [the] service."[1]

Another person who contacted the Bureau of Pensions on Edward's behalf was William Cogswell, the man responsible for forming Company C of the 2nd Massachusetts Infantry Volunteers Regiment. After President Lincoln's initial call for troops, Cogswell had turned his new Salem, Massachusetts, law practice into a recruiting office. Edward Augustus Phalen of Salem joined up. Cogswell would later serve terms as mayor of Salem and represented Massachusetts in the U.S. House of Representatives from 1887 to 1895.[2]

Cogswell already had given a sworn affidavit as to Edward's having been in his unit when the first application for a disability pension was filed in 1867.[3] Later, in an 1890 affidavit to a notary public in the District of Columbia, then-Congressman Cogswell affirmed that as captain of Company C he had been acquainted with Edward and knew that he had been a victim of malaria on certain dates. Cogswell's comments referred to events in the spring of 1862, when federal troops under Union Major General Nathaniel S.P. Banks were retreating after a defeat by Confederate soldiers serving under Major General Thomas "Stonewall" Jackson. Cogswell's recollection offers a vivid picture of the conditions Edward and his compatriots endured during a mission at Winchester, Virginia.[4]

The notary's report explains:

On this fourth day of September, A.D., 1890, personally appeared before me, a Notary Public in and for the above named District, duly authorized to administer oaths, William Cogswell, aged 51 years, a resident of Salem, in the County of Essex and State of Massachusetts, who being duly sworn according to law, states that he is acquainted with Edward A. Phalen, applicant for increase of Invalid pension, and knows the said Phalen to be the identical person of that name who enlisted as a private in Co. C, Second Regiment of Massachusetts Volunteers, and who was disabled at Winchester, Va. on or about the 23rd day of May, 1862, by reason of disability resulting from Malarial poisoning, as follows.

> He was unable to do his duty properly as a soldier, and was obliged to be assisted and cared for by the members of his company. That the facts stated are personally known to the affiant by reason of the fact that he was at that time Captain of said Co. C, Second Massachusetts Volunteer Infantry, and that Edward A. Phalen was First Sergeant of said Company; that the said regiment was covering the retreat of Bank's [sic] army during the night of May 22nd; that said company C acted as skirmishers during the night, and had a long and tedious march through the damp grain, over walls and fences and through ditches, being under continuous fire for several hours; that on arrival at Winchester, early in the morning of May 23rd, the company was detailed on outpost duty; that on arrival at the outpost Sergeant Phalen lay down in the grass, where he remained until we were driven back in our line of battle an hour or two later, when we found him unable to rise, by reason of stiffness in his limbs, and were obliged to assist him to his feet and back to our new position on the line of battle, where he was obliged to be cared for, and was unable to move about, as his position required him to do, and I desired him to seek a hospital in town, but he declared himself unable to go so far.
>
> This disability we attributed to Neuralgia or Rheumatism, arising from Malaria, from which many men were then suffering.

Another affidavit in support of Edward came from Dennis Mehan, who identified himself as Late Capt. Company F of the 2nd Regiment Massachusetts Volunteer Infantry. He, too, remembered Edward's May 1862 malaria attack, as well as other times that Edward was similarly afflicted. In one such instance, a sick Edward apparently crossed paths with a gentleman who became a U.S. President, Benjamin Harrison.[5] Mehan's affidavit:

Officer's Certificate of Disability

I, Dennis Mehan Late Captain of Company F of the Second Regiment of Mass. Vol. Inft., certify on honor that the said Capt. E.A. Phalen is the identical person of that name who volunteered as a private in Co. C 2nd Regt. Mass Vol. Inft. And who was disabled during the war, on account of disability resulting from Malaria and chills and fever. The facts here stated are personally know [sic] to me by reason of the fact that I was personally acquainted with said Phalen during the entire war, first as a private and non-commissioned officer in Co. C, 1st Lieut. and capt. in said regiment; that I remember his incurring from this cause at or near_____Va., May 22 and 23, 1862, and being unable to perform his duty in consequence thereof. That I was with him on detached service in November & December 1864, and January & February 1865, that while on said detached service I called to see him near Scottsboro, Alabama while on the March, and found him in bed at Col [sic] Harrison's headquarters near that place, suffering from Malaria,_____disabled, where he remained several days sleeping with the Colonel (now President Harrison.) I know him as suffering from chills and fever several times during the war, but do not recall dates, except the last one which was in January 1865. As far as I know, he was in good health at time of enlistment.

The testimony about Edward's malaria did not convince seeming bureaucrats of the era to move with any haste on the pension-increase request. Months after Dr. Carlson, Cogswell and Mehan had testified, Edward was still making his plea for the legitimacy of a pension raise. An affidavit bearing his signature offers a poignant summation of his health, a picture of battlefield medicine at the time, and a glimpse into the spirit of the man.[6] To the authorities handling his case Edward wrote:

Salem, Mass., March 16, 1891

I hereby certify that the malarial poisoning upon which my claim for additional pension is based, was contracted sometime previous to May 24th, 1862, but exactly when it is impossible for me to state. I was several times dosed with quinine and whiskey by the surgeon, but as the then surgeon is dead, as are several of his successors, I am unable to obtain a certificate from him or them. I was never treated for the same in a hospital, nor for anything else except wounds, when other, and, as I considered, more important matters occupied my attention.

Unfortunately, as it seems, I have no hospital record, but I still continue to have malaria, blood poisoning, neuralgia, piles, etc., as stated in my claim, and have had these troubles almost without intermission since May, 1862.

Edward A. Phalen

A memo of the Bureau of Pensions indicates that Congressman Cogswell remained interested in Edward's request. It notes that "Hon. Wm. Cogswell called up this case March 20, 1891, and should be informed of its adjudication."[7]

On April 23, 1891, Edward's physician, Dr. Carlson, again had to offer testimony about Edward's health. Among other physical ailments, he wrote, "He has enlargement of spleen and liver the result of malarial disease." His conclusion: "I consider his case a serious one and a question of [a] short-time when he will be totally disabled."

Almost a year later, on March 2, 1892, Dr. Carlson provided another affidavit noting that Edward "had an attack of brain trouble Feb. 29. I found him with partial paralysis of left side and aphasia—He is now totally disabled from all work—I believe his disease is rapidly progressing."[8]

Also on March 2, 1892, Edward's wife, Anna, aged 47, and his sister Mary A. Phalen [a.k.a. Maryanne Phalen], aged 56, offered testimony before Justice of the Peace Albion M. Dudley about Edward's much-deteriorated health and the family's economic dilemma.[9] Paraphrasing their comments, Dudley wrote that Maryanne was called to the house of her brother on February 29, 1892, and found him in an unconscious condition with his forehead and eye bruised and swollen as the result of falling from his chair. The women attested to his being confined to a bed with incoherent speech and needing the assistance of both of them and his son to be moved. Maryanne's testimony notes that because of "said soldier's inability to earn a proper support for his family she [his wife] finds herself in necessitous circumstances and is compelled to accept monetary assistance beyond that received from her husband's pension money which is now only seventeen dollars per month."

The money Anna was compelled to accept was the six dollars a month Edward had been receiving from a military relief organization in Salem beginning in September of 1889.[10] The matter of this aid and Edward's health and economic circumstances had been offered as testimony, likely meant for the Bureau of Pensions, by one William F.M. Collins before a justice of the peace on March 22, 1891, a year before Anna gave her own testimony.

Identifying himself as "clerk of the committee on military aid" in Salem, Collins said Edward was in "very needy circumstances and [in the] condition of being totally disabled from performing any kind of labor whatever on account of paralysis and brain trouble and requires the constant attendance of a nurse to care for him. That he is at present wholly dependent upon said aid and a United States pension of seventeen dollars per month for support. That said pension and aid are inadequate for his support and maintenance and that he is in danger of becoming a public charge if said pension is not soon increased."[11]

By March of 1892, Edward's son, William C. Phalen, who at some point became a stenographer like his father, sent a note to Congressman Cogswell informing him of his dad's worsening health and pointing out that the pension increase request still was unresolved.[12]

> *March 3rd, 1892*
>
> *Hon. Wm. Cogswell, Washington, D.C.*
> *Dear Sir: —*
> *I write to inform you that my father has just had the third shock of paralysis, and is now totally disabled. Dr. A.M. Dudley has taken affidavits as to his condition, and probably they may hurry up his claim a little.*
>
> *Yours very truly,*
> *W.C. Phalen*

Dudley, this same day, wrote to Cogswell, addressing him by his honorary military title, and spoke of the affidavits.[13]

> *My dear General:*
> *At the request of Mrs. Phalen I called at her house yesterday and obtained the enclosed affidavits which she desired me to forward to you in the hope that with them you might get his [Edward's] application for increase acted upon at once. He was examined on the 10th by the Lynn [Massachusetts] Board and their report must now be before the Dept. at Washington. Phalen has failed very rapidly and I do not think he can hold out much longer. He has not been able to do any work at all now*

for a long time and I do not think he ever will be able to again.
Very truly,
A.M. Dudley

A memo of the Bureau of Pensions indicates that Congressman Cogswell had taken notice of the letters from Edward's son and Dudley and had contacted the bureau. The memo notes that "Hon. W. Cogswell called up this case March 7, 1892, and should be informed of its adjudication."[14]

Even with a member of Congress in Edward's "court," the wheels of the government agency responsible for granting or denying a pension increase continued to turn—or wobble—slowly; and, as with bureaucracies of today, things got miserably overlooked, in the form of a letter lost or buried on a desk, perhaps, for nearly six months. On November 28, 1892, Thomas D. Ingram, a referee working with the medical division of the Department of the Interior, Bureau of Pensions, wrote to Edward's physician, Dr. C.A. Carlson.[15] He noted:

Dear Doctor:
In a letter written by you June 10, 1892, just handed me for consideration by General Cogswell, you say that you have been the attendant of Edward A. Phalon [sic], late Captain of Co. B, 2nd Mass. Vols., since 1876, and that your observation of his case has led you to believe that his disability is due to exposure in the service, together with malarial poisoning contracted there.

Ingram's letter goes on to note that a medical examination of Edward performed by a surgeon associated with the Bureau of Pensions medical department on April 5, 1892, after he had an attack of partial unconsciousness, in February, had found no evidence of malarial disease. *It is desired that you furnish this office a full clinical history of his case, explaining, if possible, any pathological relationship connecting his malarial poisoning with the condition ending in disease of brain and hemiplegia. It is believed that you alone are best* [the word "best" was crossed out by an unknown party] *prepared to give us a correct history of this man's disabilities.*
Very respectfully,
Thos. D. Ingram
Medical referee

Weeks later, on January 2, 1893, in a long handwritten letter to Thomas Ingram, Dr. Carlson acknowledged Ingram's letter of November 28, 1892. He said that Edward's condition "is one of total disability, requiring the constant care of an attendant both day and night." He further said, "He cannot get from bed to chair, walk or stand without help. He has to be catheterized and [his] rectum cleared by attendant." He repeated earlier testimony that the enlargement of liver and spleen were "primarily due to malarial disease," and that the "hemiplegia and brain disease is clearly the result of arterial degeneration, and I believe the pathological relationship between the brain disease and malarial poisoning is thus fully established."[16]

One might ask why or how it was that a letter written by Edward's doctor June 10, 1892, explaining once again that he had been caring for him for the past sixteen years, "just got handed" to the medical referee by Cogswell six months later. On whose desk had it sat? Someone in Cogswell's own office, or in a basket at the Bureau of Pensions?

Incredible as it may seem, eight days after Dr. Carlson answered Ingram, a report dated January 10, 1893, shows that the medical referee requested that Edward be examined again.[17]

Ultimately, on February 25, 1893, the Medical Division of the Bureau of Pensions reported that "in view of the evidence in this case, the statements of the attending physician and members of the boards of examining surgeons with their description of the conditions formed, it is believed that the disease of nervous system, now existing, is the result of malarial poisoning, contracted while in the military service."[18]

Edward A. Phalen died at age fifty-three and eight months on April 15, 1894, due to cerebral thrombosis secondary to malaria, his death certificate noted.[19] Another physician, Dr. Hardy Phippen, who had been treating Edward from January 1893 until his death, said that Edward suffered episodes of paralysis, bouts of severe chills, and had been "bed-ridden" for the last ten years before he passed away.[20] An obituary in the *Boston Journal* stated that he had served in the 2nd Massachusetts Regiment in Company C, "was promoted to Captain" and had worked as a stenographer.[21]

Nowhere, however, is it stated what Edward endured as a man involved in the brutal Civil War or how poorly this veteran was treated in its aftermath, for a disability pension raise from seventeen to twenty-four dollars a month.

POSTSCRIPT

Michael William Phalen and his brother Edward lived to see an exciting era of achievement, one that their Irish immigrant grandfather, Maurice Phelan, born about seventy years before them, scarcely could have imagined. This patriarch of the Phalen family might well have said that Michael and Edward, two grandsons he did not live long enough to meet, brought his dream of a better life full circle in that place called America—and that they were wise to fight for a country in which the Irish would one day thrive and be respected. One has only to witness the contributions of the Irish in all walks of life to see that this has occurred—from business professionals to teachers, from gallant members of law enforcement to firefighters, from mayors to politicians at the highest levels, including an Irish Catholic U.S. president.

"Now, who would have believed it?" you can almost hear Maurice, Edward and Michael say with smiles.

epilogue

Bill Phalen found the burial site of his Civil War veteran great-granduncle, Edward Augustus Phalen, and Edward's wife, Anna, at Greenlawn Cemetery in Salem, Massachusetts. Not noted on the monument, the couple's son William also is interred there.

Bill Phalen took this photograph at Holy Cross Cemetery in Halifax, Nova Scotia, where his great-great grandfather, who died in 1847, is buried. What likely was a wooden grave marker would long since have disintegrated. The cemetery, which opened in 1843, is said to have been the final resting place of about 23,000 souls, many of whom, like Bill's immigrant family, were of Irish descent.

Civil War veteran Michael William Phalen purchased what beame a family plot at Calvary Catholic Cemetery near Chicago in 1868. He, two of his wives and several very young children of Michael's who perished were interred there, as well as other family members over the years.

William Joseph Phalen, Bill Phalen's grandfather, was the only surviving child from the marriage of Michael William Phalen and his second wife, Margaret "Maggie" Phalen.

Michael William Phalen was married to third wife Mary Curtin Phalen for thirty-four years.

Some Reflections From Bill Phalen

M*y ancestors, and what I discovered...*A visitor to Halifax, Nova Scotia, today will see some of the same sights my great-great-great grandfather, Maurice Phelan, and his sons saw when they got off their ship at Halifax during the first half of the 19th century: a clock tower built in the early 1800s, and the historic Citadel fortress atop a hill. These are part of Halifax's historic treasures.

What cannot be seen is the cemetery where Irish Catholic Maurice was interred in 1837. Also part of the city's history, the location is something the Catholic Church in Halifax would rather not talk about, I believe, a secretive subject and a cause for shame.

I tried to find out where Maurice's burial site was when I visited the city a few years back. I went to Halifax's St. Mary's Cathedral Basilica, which early in the city's history—before splendid revisions—had been named St.Peter's Church.

A priest I happened on in a St. Mary's parking lot said he had no information about where my relative might be interred, and advised me to contact the church's administration for such history. A St. Mary's clerk advised me to seek out early church records, which, unfortunately, I was advised, were no longer kept at St. Mary's. I did learn over time—through other sources that held old St. Peter's and St. Mary's church records—that Maurice had indeed died in 1837 in Halifax, but that was all. Exactly where he was buried seemed swept away.

It would be years before I could begin to make any sense out of the mystery of where my family patriarch ancestor's remains lay—and that, I learned, could very well be under the parking lot where I had stopped the priest for information. I could have been standing on Maurice's asphalt-covered grave. I am not happy about it, and neither would he be, I expect.

How did I find out where he and thousands of others are entombed? An Internet search in 2013, when this narrative was first being put together, turned up information based on a newspaper opinion piece published in Halifax's *The Chronicle Herald* the year before [*The Chronicle Herald*, "Respecting Memory of Church's Founders," June 23, 2012]. That news also was reported by the Canadian Broadcasting Corporation the same day ["Halifax Church Expansion Could Affect Hidden Graves," CBC News, June 23, 2012].

It was a St. Mary's parishioner who alerted the media with his fear that a then-proposed church expansion project would further disturb graves already hidden under a church parking lot. That was St. Peter's graveyard, in use from the 1780s to when a new cemetery, Holy Cross, opened in 1843. (Maurice's son Lawrence, my great-great grandfather, I learned, died in 1847 and was buried at Holy Cross.)

The concerned citizen wrote the newspaper: "Most of the early worshippers of St. Peter's were Irish immigrants and their descendants, together with the Mi'kmaq community and [a]scattering of Scots, German and English Catholics." Grave markers, he said, were either made of wooden boards or stone. Many of the Irish were struggling laborers or lower-middle-class citizens, he explained, so the majority of their graves were noted by wooden markers, which had deteriorated over time and disappeared. Of the stone markers, he told CBC News, "When Holy Cross was opened, some of the more well-to-do families moved some of the headstones and some of the remains to Holy Cross, but the majority were left behind."

Maurice would have had a grave marker of wood, I think, because it is doubtful that my Irish immigrant relatives could have afforded stone during that time of hardship. The parishioner's newspaper piece noted that by the 1950s "the old graveyard was paved over, sealing in the remains of 2,000 men, women and children."

That number is closer to three-thousand burials, according to another source, genealogical historian and author Terrence M. Punch. In his book "Erin's Sons: Irish Arrivals in Atlantic Canada, 1761-1853," Punch wrote: "The earliest Catholic parish of St. Peter's Church, which became St. Mary's Basilica, had an adjacent burial ground. The records of burials only began in 1800, and the cemetery, having been closed in 1843 and paved over as a schoolyard in the 20th century, there is no physical evidence to be seen of the resting place of three-thousand people, many of them natives of Ireland."[1] The name Maurice Phelan was included in the book as one of them. At this writing, the proposed expansion project had not moved forward, I learned.

There is, I suppose, some small comfort in knowing that my great-great-great grandfather was in good company. Even a member of 15th-century British royalty did not have it any better than he did. The bones of King Richard III were discovered under a parking lot in central England in 2012. Scientists were busy scanning his bones, creating replicas of his crooked spine to pinpoint scoliosis. If they did the same for Maurice Phelan, they would find the spirit of an Irishman of true grit, I think.

Deciding to emigrate from his very poor but familiar homeland, he gave future generations of his kin the chance for opportunity. As was written in previous chapters, we know more of what happened to family members when they made the United States their home than during their years spent in Nova Scotia.

MOVING TO THE UNITED STATES

In America, this land of opportunity, the family ultimately would thrive. Maurice's daughter-in-law, Ann Johnston Phalen, bringing her family to Massachusetts after her husband's death, saw her children grow up and join the country's mainstream, with two sons, Michael and Edward, fighting for their new land in the Civil War. Ann died in 1885 of cancer and is buried in an unmarked grave—lot 54 on Lake Avenue—at St. Mary's Catholic Cemetery in Salem, Massachusetts; the lot number in cemetery records fails to tell the story of this brave, adventurous mother. She is a long way from her husband, Lawrence, who died 38 years before her in 1847 and was interred in Halifax, Nova Scotia's Holy Cross Cemetery. If there was a grave marker for him, it likely was of wood and is long gone. I did not see any marker when I visited the cemetery.

Ann Johnston Phalen was living at 63 Mason Street in Salem at the time of her death. She was not alone. Her daughter, Marianne Phalen, who appears to have remained single, was boarding at the same address, as noted in Salem city directories beginning in 1879, through to 1916. A dressmaker, she moved to Boston.[2] No further information about her was found.

Michael, my great-grandfather, had fathered nine children. Sadly, only three survived to grow into manhood—one of them, fortunately, being William Joseph Phalen, my grandfather. Michael is interred with his second and third wives, Margaret "Maggie" Ryan Phalen and Mary H. Curtin Phalen, at Calvary Cemetery in Evanston, Illinois. With Margaret, he had five children, with only my grandfather living to adulthood; with Mary he had four children, and only two sons lived on as my grandfather's half brothers. Many of Michael's offspring—including my grandfather—and other family members are buried at Calvary Cemetery. There are a few small stone grave markers there, one of them bearing Michael's name—fitting, for it was he who bought the family plot not long after the Civil War. A name carved in stone among many Civil War-era graves at this old cemetery cannot even hint at my veteran relative's riveting and patriotic past.

His Civil War veteran brother, Edward, and Edward's wife, Anna M. Sherwood Phalen, lived at 39 Boardman in Salem, Massachusetts, at the time of Edward's death in 1894. She died in 1917. They were laid to rest at Salem's Greenlawn Cemetery. An elegant stone monument has their carved names and dates they lived. Records show that their son, William, was interred there as well, but his name did not make it to the gravestone. Anna is recorded as having purchased the plot. The dignified monument does not tell of Edward's wartime bravery, his wounds and the effects they had on his health the rest of his life.

THE WIDOWS—AND WHAT THEY FACED

So much time has passed since the Civil War. But some things seem to remain the same. Just as veterans of wars today have faced off with bungling bureaucrats—as in the Veterans Administration terrible scandals of 2014—my great-grandfather, Michael, and his brother, Edward, had their own postwar battles. As our story related, they had to endure numerous obstacles when applying for U.S. Civil War pension payments promised them by the government. Adding insult to injury, after their deaths, their wives, too, faced roadblocks when applying to the Department of Interior Bureau of Pensions for widows' pensions.[3]

Edward's wife of twenty-five years, Anna M. Sherwood Phalen, had to prove that she indeed was married to him and when and where this event had occurred. This necessitated several sworn affidavits from those who knew the couple, and, one can imagine, caused a series of annoyances. For example, after twenty-five years of marriage, and raising a son with Edward, she had to locate the person who had married the couple in her hometown of Dayton, Ohio. That gentleman, M. Huston, Minister of the Gospel, on April 28, 1894, certified that he had "solemnized the marriage"

June 17, 1869. The Commonwealth of Massachusetts, too, was called on for substantiation, and on May 14, 1894, the Salem City Clerk provided a record of the couple's "Intentions of Marriage," originally proposed for June 14, 1869. Anna did get her widow's pension, but not without inconveniences.

Michael's third wife, Mary H. Curtin Phalen, was married to my great-grandfather for thirty-four years before he died on March 14, 1908; she, too, had to offer the Bureau of Pensions proof of marriage when seeking her widow's pension but was unable to locate either a public or church record of matrimony. Moving to Buffalo, New York, not long after Michael's death, she advised the Bureau of Pensions that she and Michael had been married in New York City by a Catholic priest, but that she could not recall the church, the name of the priest who married them, or names of witnesses at the ceremony. She turned to those who knew her best for assistance.

In May of 1908, her son Charles Phalen and his half brother (my grandfather) William Joseph Phalen were witnesses on an affidavit for the Bureau of Pensions that noted Mary H. [for Helen] Curtin Phalen as the "identical person" she said she was. Then, in July of that year, the men were witnesses when she gave a law firm the power of attorney to act in her behalf in obtaining a widow's pension. Charles was twenty-four and my grandfather thirty-six, according to their testimony.

Michael's married sisters, Margaret Phalen Savory and Ellen (also known as Elinor or Eleanor) Phalen Dalton, both living in Massachusetts, signed affidavits that they were certain of their brother's third marriage to sister-in-law Mary H. Curtin Phalen. (A year after Michael died, his sister Margaret passed away.)[4] Mary H. Curtin Phalen either did not know or had forgotten that she was Michael's third wife, apparently until she read her sisters-in-law's affidavits. Likely to avoid any problems in her widow's pension moving forward, and probably on the advice of her lawyer, she wrote the following in a signed affidavit to the Bureau of Pensions. "In my application for pension under Act of April 19, 1908, I stated soldier was married once before me. This statement is incorrect as I have learned he was married twice before me. ... The evidence of soldier's two sisters is the best obtainable as to the death of the first wife."

A combination of her possible memory issues and the Bureau of Pension's slowness stalled her widow's pension-request process. Finally, ten months after Michael's death, in a January 1909 affidavit, in which Mary

H. Curtin Phalen noted her age as 60, she wrote: "The evidence on file of witnesses showing our cohabitation as man and wife from time of my marriage in 1874 to date of death is best obtainable proof of fact of marriage." Through her lawyer, she eventually did receive a twelve-dollars-a-month widow's pension, retroactive to April 1908.

However, in 1917, when she sought an age-related pension increase, it appeared that memory had clouded her true age. Reviewing her request for an increase in her widow's pension, the Bureau of Pensions noted an inconsistency and demanded proof of her age. In her 1909 affidavit, she had reported that she was 60. That put her age at the time of her 1917 request at 68; she did not meet the age qualification under a new law [Act of September 8, 1916] that would have given her a pension of fifty dollars a month if she had been age 70.

She wrote the bureau that she had turned 70 but had learned that records of her birth had been lost. "My cousin who lives in Milwaukee went to the old church where I was baptized but found that the records of birth had many years ago been transferred to St. Johns Cathedral. In looking them over, although she found the records of other members of my family, unfortunately mine was not amongst them. The Pastor explained to her that many were lost in course of transferring. As there is no other proof of my birth that I ever knew of, I can only give you my word that I was 70 years old the eighth of last April." In another letter to the Bureau of Pensions, she expressed her insult at being doubted. Her husband, she said, "was one of the bravest men that fought during the Civil War and I feel the humiliation more than I can express that his old widow's word should be doubted or that she would stoop to perjury to gain the small advantage that she is entitled to."

Although she did not qualify for that particular pension increase, Mary H. Curtin Phalen, who outlived her husband by twenty years, was receiving a forty-dollars-a-month widow's pension before she died on October 15, 1928. After her death, her son Frank, on November 26, 1928, wrote to the Bureau of Pensions, advising the agency of his mother's death, and asking where he should return her latest pension check.

All of the correspondence and affidavits associated with both Michael and Edward Phalen and their wives were discovered in military, medical and pension records maintained by the National Archives and Records Administration.

While it is the better part of a century since Michael's and Edward's wives were concerned about their widows' pensions, a recent news report brought the aftermath of the 19th-century Civil War into modern times. A headline in the weekend section of *The Wall Street Journal* dated May 10-11, 2014, read: "The Civil War's Last Pensioner." The story surrounded the last child of a Civil War veteran who was still receiving pension money. She was the daughter of a man who had "joined the rebels, deserted on the road to Gettysburg, defected to the Union and married so late in life to a woman so young that their daughter Irene is today 84 years old—and the last child of any Civil War veteran still on the VA benefits rolls."

The government kept its pension promise in the above quirky case, as it eventually did for Mary H. Curtin Phalen and Anna M. Sherwood Phalen. This is a good country, after all, despite some in government positions who are not so good.

Looking back, our family has taken a circuitous journey over the nearly two centuries since Maurice Phelan and his sons boarded a ship in poverty-stricken Ireland that was headed for Halifax, Nova Scotia, and the unknown. After a spell, my forebears wandered down to the United States—first to Salem, Massachusetts, then Chicago, Illinois, and, in the here and now, to Phoenix, Arizona, fulfilling the American Dream.

addendum

Michael William Phalen
1842–1908

A Memorial For A Civil War Veteran

 member of the Illinois Commandery of the Military Order of the Loyal Legion of the United States (MOLLUS), my great-grandfather, U.S. Civil War Union Army veteran Michael William Phalen, was honored with this MOLLUS memorial. It appears here exactly as it was written, with no mention of his first wife, who died when he was a young man engaged in war. Presumably based in part on information Michael would have provided his compatriots in advance of his passing, the touching tribute notes that he moved to Massachusetts in 1848. He was then six years old.

MICHAEL WILLIAM PHALEN
Michael William Phalen, born September 4, 1842, at Halifax, Nova Scotia, died March 14, 1908 at Chicago, Ill.

Salem, Mass., became his home in 1848 and there on April 7, 1861 he enlisted as a Union Soldier, giving his age as twenty-one, lest on account of his youth he should fail to be accepted. He was mustered in as First Sergeant of Co. F 9th Regiment Massachusetts Infantry Volunteers June 1, 1861, as Second Lieutenant Sept. 7, 1861, as First Lieutenant Jan. 28, 1862, appointed Adjutant of that regiment Aug. 28, 1862, and honorably discharged for expiration of term of service, June 21, 1864.

He was elected an Original Companion of the First Class of the Military Order of the Loyal Legion of the United States through the commandery of the State of Illinois, February 14, 1895.

His regiment, which by reason of its valor in many severe engagements earned the soubriquet of "The Bloody Ninth," was organized June 11, 1861 and it is recorded that on that day at Faneuil Hall in the City of Boston "First Sergeant Michael W. Phalen gave an exhibition drill of his company (F), a fine appearing and uniformed body of young and stalwart men, then recently arrived from Salem and called the Fitzgerald Guards in honor of Lord Edward Fitzgerald the Irish patriot and martyr." This regiment reached Washington June 29, 1861, and encamping in that vicinity was held there in reserve during the battle of Bull Run, July 21, 1861. On the 23rd they marched into Virginia encamping near Fort Corcoran and being assigned to the Brigade of Gen. William Tecumseh Sherman. This Brigade, on the Corps organization of the army became the 2nd Brigade, 1st Division, 5th Army Corps of the Army of the Potomac and under General Fitzjohn Porter. Morrell and others achieved remarkable distinction on many a well-fought field.

The history of the 9th Massachusetts is that of Companion Phalen. Passing the autumn and winter of 1861-2 in drill, guard, picket and re-connoitering duty in presence of the enemy then confronting Washington they became well equipped for the approaching conflicts of that great army. Transferred to the Peninsula with the Army of the Potomac in the spring of 1862, young Phalen was an active participant in the following affairs, skirmishes and battles; viz., Siege of Yorktown, April 5 to May 4, 1862; West Point, New Bridge, Hanover C.H., Mechanicsville, Gaines Mill, White Oak Swamp, Malvern Hill, Rappahannock Sta., Manassas, South Mountain, Antietam, Sharpsburg, Boettler's Mills, Shepardstown, Fredericksburg, Chancellorsville, Ely's Ford, Brandy Sta., Aldie Gap, Gettysburg, Wapping Heights, Rappahannock Sta., Locust Grove, Mine Run, Wilderness, Laurel Hill, Po River, Spottsylvania, North Anna, Shady Grove, Bethesda Church and Cold Harbor, June 5, 1864. The three-year term of service then expiring the regiment left "the front" and was honorably discharged at Boston, Mass., June 21, 1864. Adjutant Phalen was wounded in the forehead by a piece of shell at Gaines Mill May 29, 1862 and was struck on the hip by an unexploded and ricochetting shell at Mine Run, Nov. 29, 1863, but on either occasion, left the field only for the time required to dress his wounds. A companion who served with him in the 9th writes of him as follows: "Phalen distinguished himself by conspicuous gallantry at the battle of Malvern Hill. He was with his regiment in every engagement. Neatness, precision and order characterized him in the discharge of details of his office; everything was in its proper place and attended to at the proper time. His exertion and example, his promptitude and fidelity to duty went far towards creating that discipline and good name for his regiment of which we were all so proud."

In war a brave, faithful and efficient soldier; in family relations a tender and devoted husband and father; in the business world an honest and upright citizen, Companion Phalen will be deeply mourned by all who knew him.

Companion Phalen was twice married; first, to Margaret Ryan at Salem, Mass., Aug 20 [August 22], 1864, of whom was born William J. Phalen, now a reputable business man residing at Chicago and four other children who died young; second, to Mary Curtin who survives him with their two sons, Frank and Charles.

Companion Phalen was an esteemed Comrade of Geo. H. Thomas Post No. 5, Department of Illinois of the Grand Army of the Potomac.

He was a member of the Western Society of the Army of the Potomac and in the year 1906 served as its efficient secretary.

He was National Chairman of the Railway Committee of the Traveller's Protective Association, much of its success in promoting the interests of its members being due to his careful, methodical and earnest work.

Soon after the war Companion Phalen settled in Chicago and engaged in the hide and leather business in which he was successful until the great fire of Oct. 1871 swept away both business and his modest fortune. He then established himself in the same business line at Boston, Mass., only to be interrupted in a prosperous career by the great fire of Nov. 1872. He then engaged in the iron and steel trade in Chicago, becoming Secretary and Manager of the Chas. H. Gurney Company. On the retirement of that concern from the business world in 1897 he bcame the Chicago representative of Atha and Illingsworth [sic] Steel Company and on the formation of its successor, the Crucible Steel Company, Companion Phalen retired from active business, retaining the respect and esteem of all his associates.

To the bereaved wife and children this Commandery tenders its profound and sincere sympathy.

George B. Herenden,
William L. Cadle,
Roswell H. Mason,
Committee.

addendum: medical

SURGEON'S CERTIFICATE

IN CASE OF

Michael W. Phalen

Co.____, **9th.** Reg't **Mass.Vol.Inf.**

APPLICANT FOR_____ Increase

No. **1,113,889**

DATE OF EXAMINATION:

January 2nd._____, 190 7.

} BOARD.

Pres.,

Sec'y,

Treas.,

Post office, **Chicago**

County, ____ **Cook**

State, ____ **Illinois**

. **Do not use backs of certificates for any purpose other than indicated by printed matter thereon.**   6—552 b

Civil War veteran Michael William Phalen underwent a series of medical examinations over several years in an effort to secure pension benefits and increases. This 1907 record came from the National Archives and Records Administration.

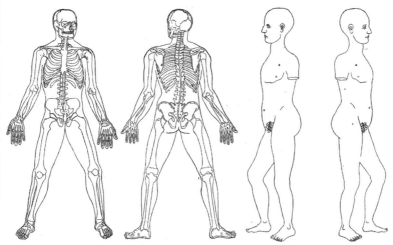

The outlines of the human skeleton and figure should be used to indicate precisely the location of a disease or injury, the entrance and exit of a missile, an amputation, etc.

(Paste continuation sheet, if used, here.)

In consideration of wounds or ailments that postwar pension-seekers might have had, a notation on this old-time medical chart states the following: "The outlines of the human skeleton and figure should be used to indicate precisely the location of a disease or injury, the entrance and exit of a missile, an amputation, etc."

MY GREAT-GRANDFATHER'S HEALTH

octors *always ask about a patient's medical history. While many can recite the status of their parents' health in their later years, few of us can recall our grand-father's specific ailments, much less our great-grandfather's. I had a look into my great-grandfather's physical condition through medical records kept by the Department of Interior Bureau of Pensions. My great-grandfather, Civil War veteran Michael William Phalen, underwent required physical examinations over the years in which he applied for a postwar government pension. The notes from the examinations and the progress of his requests were discovered in records made available by the National Archives and Records Administration. I even learned that my ancestor's eyes were hazel in color, a detail I was able to provide artist Russ Recchion when he asked what color he should paint Michael's eyes for the very fine portrait he painted of him!*
—Bill Phalen

MEDICAL REPORTS OF MICHAEL WILLIAM PHALEN

1900
Surgeon's Certificate [Doctors A.W. [not clear] Gray, James Burry and I.V. [not clear] Luse were the board physicians]
[Character of pension claim:] Original
Pension Claim No. 1.103.633
Name of claimant: Michael W. Phalen
1st Lieut. Company F Reg't. Mass. Inf.
Claimant's post-office address: 10 S. Canal St., Chicago

Address of Board: Chicago P.O., Ill.
Date of examination: March 30, 1900

[Cause of disability:] Wound of head. Rheumatism. Disease of urinary organs.

[Claimant's statement:] He makes the following statement upon which he bases his claim for original [invalid pension request].

Rheumatism all over - in left shoulder and side especially. G.S. wound of head does not trouble him. No disease of urinary organs. Has indigestion.

We hereby certify that upon examination we find the following objective conditions: Pulse rate [sitting, standing, after exercise], 80. 80. 110, respiration, 16. 16. 29, temperature, 98.6, height, 5 feet 10 1/2 inches; actual weight, 226 pounds; age 57 years.

G.S. wound of head: At margin of hair in center of forehead is a small superficial scar - not tender, dragging or adherent. No depression of bone. No evidence of diseased condition of brain or membranes. No vertigo, spasms, convulsions or nausea. No local or general _____. No hemiplegia or paraplegia. Mental condition sound.

_____ Not rated.

Rheumatism: Shoulders and knees crepitant. Lumbar muscles sore. No enlarged, swollen, tender or stiff parts. No limitation of motion. No atrophy or contraction of muscles or tendons. Heart normal in size, position, sounds, force and rhythm. No murmurs. No dyspnoea, oedema, cyanosis.

Rated six-eighteenths.

Urinary organs: Urine acid clear, sp.gr. 1020. No albumen. No sugar. No blood, pus or sediment. No cystitis or urethritis. No strictures.

_____ Not rated.

Tongue clean. Skin of healthy color. Liver and spleen normal. No abdominal tenderness. No noted disease. Nutrition and muscular development good.

_____ Not rated.

Salesman. Palms soft. No evidence of vicious habits. No other disability is found to exist.

1905

Surgeon's Certificate [doctors James Burry and H.M. Stowe were the board physicians]

Character of pension claim: Original

Pension Claim No. 1103.633,

Name of claimant: Michael W. Phalen

Company 9 Reg't Mass V.I.

Claimant's post-office address: 1580 Kenmore Ave., Chicago

Address of Board: Chicago P.O., Ill.

Date of examination: July 29, 1905

Names of disabilities: Rheumatism, heart _____ stomach, deafness, impaired vision

Claimant's statement: He makes the following statement in regard to the origin of his disabilities and date when first discovered by him: I have had rheumatism 15 years. Disease of heart I disclaim. I have intentinal [intestinal?] trouble for 5 years, have lost 25 pounds in 3 months. I have been deaf in left ear 4 years. I have worn glasses 10 years.

Birthplace, Halifax, N.S.; age, 62 years; height, 5-9; weight, 200 pounds; complexion, dark; color of eyes, hazel; color of hair, dark gray; occupation, none; permanent marks and scars other than those described below, none.

Pulse rate, 78. 86. 98 [sitting, standing, after exercise]; respiration, 18. 20. 24 [sitting, standing, after exercise]; temperature, 98.6.

Description of disabilities: Both shoulders stiff; right shoulder crepitant. Gait slow, stoops and recovers with difficulty by reason of distended abdomen, Heart normal, apex beat is plain to inspection and palpation, area of cardiac dullness normal. Position, rhythm and force normal. No murmur, no dilatation or hypertrophy. No oedema, cyanosis or dyspnoea. Chest measurements 36 1/2, 35 inches. Normal resonance at all points. No cough, rales or expectoration. No pleuritic exudate or adhesions. No disease of lungs.

No emaciation, general debility, number of movements and character of stools normal. Eyes murky, skin clear, tongue brown coated. Teeth in bad condition, foul odor. Marked rumbling. Abdomen distended, liver one inch below arch, spleen normal, frequent eructations of gas. No pile tumors, Stomach and colon are distended with gas. Stomach tender on pressure. Abdomen measures 45 inches.

Deafness— Both Eustachian tubes closed. Left ear drum reddened, inflammed. Light reflex absent, no perforation. Soldier can hear ordinary conversation at 3 feet, but cannot at six feet with left ear. Right ear normal. Can hear ordinary conversation at eight feet, right ear.

Eyes — V. 20/70, corrected to 20/40. No disease of lids. Retinas normal. Media clear.

Sp. Gr. of urine 1020, light yellow, acid reaction. No albumen, sugar or blood. No disease of kidneys.

Senility— No arcus senilis, no tremor, skin rough. Appears to be 68 years old.

We find that the aggregate permanent disability for earning a support by manual labor is caused by rheumatism, stomach trouble, deafness and age, not due to vicious habits, and warrants a rating of $8. per month. Except as above no disability found to exist.

1907
Surgeon's Certificate [doctors James Burry, R.C. Wilson and J.R. Corbus were the board physicians]

Character of pension claim: Increase [pension request]

Pension Claim No. 1, 113, 389

Name of claimant: Michael W. Phalen

Company 9th Reg't Mass. Vol. Inf.

Claimant's post-office address: 1580 Kenmore Ave., Chicago

Address of Board: Chicago P.O., Ill.

Date of examination: January 2, 1907

Names of disabilities: Rheumatism, Disease of heart, and Stomach, Impaired vision, Deafness.

[Claimant's statement:] He makes the following statement in regard to the origin of his disabilities and date when first discovered by him: Rheumatism 10 yrs. Disease of heart 3 yrs. Disease of stomach 5yrs. Impaired vision 16 yrs. Deafness 8 yrs.

Birthplace: Halifax; age 63 years; height, 5.11 1/2; weight, 185 pounds; complexion, Dark; color of eyes, hazel; color of hair, Iron gray; occupation, Nothing; permanent marks and scars other than those described below, Mole on right breast.

We hereby certify that upon examination we find the following objective conditions: Pulse rate: 72, 86, 90 [Sitting, standing, after exercise.]; respiration, 19, 23, 24 [Sitting, standing, after exercise.]; temperature, 98.6.

Rheumatism; -Shoulders are crepitant, motion is limited 20 percent from synovial thickning [sic], there is sacro-lumbar pain, unable to stoop and recover, effort painful, knees are crepitant, motion is limited 15 percent from synovial thickning [sic] all other muscles, joints and tendons are normal, heart, apex in the normal position, no hypertrophy or dilitation, no cyanosis, dyspnea or oedema.

Disease of the stomach; -Eyes are clear, tongue is white coated, skin negative, liver and spleen normal, stomach is tender, abdomen is resonant, rectum normal, well nourished, no anaemia or cachexia.

Impaired sight V.R.&L.E 20/100, corrected to 20/30, no disease of the cornea, lids or fundus, pupils respond to light and shade.

Deafness; -Can hear ordinary conversation at six feet, no greater distance, each ear is separately tested, tubes open, tympani are normal.

Age; -Has arous senilis, looks age given, moderate sclerosis, normal reflexes, memory good, no tremor, muscles are fairly firm, hands semi-soft.

Chest, measures 38 inches exhalation, 40 inches inhalation, no disease upon auscultation, palpation or percussion.

The urine us amber, acid. Sp. Gr. I 020, no albumen or sugar by the required tests, no mucus, pus or blood.

We find that the aggregate permanent disability for earning a support by manual labor is due to Rheumatism. Disease of the stomach. Impaired vision. Deafness and age not to vicious habits and warrants a rating of $10.00 per month.

Except as described in the certificate of examination claimant is suffering from no disability.

tidbits

Michael William Phalen lived long enough to get a glimpse of what ultimately would become America's future in air flight. Taken by the Wright brothers, this early photo shows a fixed-wing airplane that the two inventors had altered in 1905 to allow the pilot to assume a sitting position and had room for a passenger. The setting is Kill Devil Hills, North Carolina. Photo courtesy of the Library of Congress.

IN GREAT-GRANDFATHER'S TIME...

1900—In Chicago (where Bill Phalen's great-grandfather lived), a quart of milk cost 6 cents; a loaf of bread 5 cents; steak, 12 cents a pound.

1902—Sears Roebuck was selling a refrigerator for $27.50; an upright piano for $59.45; a 100-bar box of soap for $2.95.

1905—1909—Some average annual earnings: Teachers, $455; state and local government workers, $695; wholesale and retail trade workers, $609.

1908—average of all industries, excluding farm workers, $564.

(From "The Value of a Dollar: Prices and Incomes in the United States, 1860-2004," Third Edition, by Scott Derks, A Universal Reference Book, Grey House Publishing, Inc.)

U.S. Census Bureau figures—population growth through the decades:

1860—the U.S. population was 31,443,321. Chicago, with 112,172 people, was number nine out of ten largest urban areas. New York City was number one with a population of 813,669.

1870—the U.S. population is 38,558,371; Chicago, with 298,977 people, is the fifth-largest urban place. New York City is number one with a population of 942, 292.

1880—the U.S population is 50,189,209; Chicago, with 503,185 people, is the fourth-largest urban place in the U.S; New York City was number one with a population of 1,206,299.

1890—the U.S. population is 62,979,766; Chicago, with 1,099,850 people, is now the second-largest urban place after New York City, which has a population of 1,515,301.

1900—the U.S. population is 76, 212, 168; Chicago, with 1,698,575, is the second-largest urban place after New York City, which has a population of 3,437,202.

As Time Goes By...

Two years after Michael William Phalen died, the 1910 U.S. Census reported the U.S. Population at 92,228,496, a twenty-one percent rise over the 1900 census; Chicago, with 2,185,283 people, was still the second-largest urban place after New York City, which had a population of 4,766,883.

In the last decade of his life, Michael would have heard of some pretty terrific things. Already around when the telephone entered the scene (1876) and the light bulb (1883), he saw such modern-age development as Kodak's Brownie camera, introduced in 1900. The first silent movie, "The Great Train Robbery," debuted in 1903; it was produced by Thomas Alva Edison (father of the light bulb), who had invented various audio and visual playback machines.

That same year might have seen Michael's spirit and imagination soaring as news spread that Orville and Wilbur Wright had successfully flown a controlled, powered and sustained heavier-than-air airplane at Kitty Hawk, North Carolina—the first to do so.

And an unbelievable future lay ahead for Michael William Phalen's descendants.

LOOKING FOR IRISH ANCESTORS: A SHORT COURSE

mericans likely have little trouble understanding that they re-side in a particular state, probably in a county in that state and in a city or town within that county.

Ireland's terminology may seem a bit more complicated to those seeking their Irish roots. Take Thomastown, where the Phelans of old resided, for example. 'Thomastown' has had various legal meanings, being at once a *townland*, consisting of sixteen statute acres, and a *Catholic parish*.[1] At least one Phelan family reference is chock-full of those sometimes confounding Irish civil/religious distinctions. For example: Maurice Phelan, Bill Phalen's great-great-great grandfather, wed Eleanor Murphy October 16, 1796, in the *Thomastown (Catholic) Parish*, County Kilkenny, Ireland. The couple may have been living in Dangan, a *townland* located in the *civil parish* of Columbkille, in the *barony* of Gowran, in County Kilkenny.[2]

These distinctions at first may seem daunting, but they can be road signs to knowledge of one's Irish ancestors, as they were in tracking the genealogy of the Phelan/Phalen family.

FINDING ONE'S WAY THROUGH IRISH RECORDS:

• *Parish*—In terms of doing Irish research, a parish is either religious, or ecclesiastical, in derivation, or civil in nature, and at times the two entities cross over each other's geographic boundaries. "The civil parish was used for land valuations, was usually smaller than the ecclesiastical one, and often had a different name," writes genealogist Angus Baxter. "There are about two-and-a-half thousand ecclesiastical parishes in the whole country."[3] As one of its methods in helping Bill Phalen, the New England Historic Genealogical Society (NEHGS) compared early records of both the civil Thomastown parish and the religious-based Thomastown Catholic Church parish to learn which people with the surnames Phelan or a derivative Whelan were related to him.

A NEHGS report, which was accompanied by illustrative map overlays, noted: "You will see that the Catholic parish of Thomastown covered a number of civil parishes, and you will see in the southern section of Thomastown Catholic parish the civil parishes of Kilfane, Thomastown and Columbkille."

• *Townland*—Used largely for levying taxes and for land valuation, a townland is the smallest recognized division of Irish land, ranging from about an acre to more than seven thousand acres.[4] Various estimates consider the number of townlands in Ireland to be as many as sixty thousand or more, each with a name, albeit a sometimes shared name; and within a given townland are many other names, possibly twenty to thirty.[5] A townland's average area is three hundred and fifty acres.[6]

• *Barony*—A barony is a territorial division of a county and is composed of a number of townlands. Baronies served as bases for taxation and other administrative functions.[7] "This division goes back into the mists of early Irish history and is based on Gaelic family holdings," according to Baxter. "There are three hundred and twenty-five baronies in all Ireland. They were turned into civil divisions by the English in the 19th century for the purpose of land valuation."[8]

Ever so simply put, information tucked within the old records of parishes, townlands and baronies can be springboards to yielding discoveries about Irish ancestors.

As one might expect, names of townlands and other locales across Ireland are in both Gaelic and English (born of the long-term British conquest); but they also reflect others who left their mark on the Emerald Isle: the ancient Celts and perhaps people before them; Vikings who sprinkled areas with Norse names; and Anglo-Normans. The latter invading group was the first to add the English suffix "town" to a place name[9], as in Thom*astown*, Bill Phalen's great-great-great-grandfather's home. The "Thomas" part is said to have come from the locale's 13th-century founder, Thomas FitzAnthony, an Anglo-Norman official.[10]

Good hunting!

End Notes

PROLOGUE

1. *Catholic Online Encyclopedia,* www.catholic.org/encyclopedia.
2. Terrence M. Punch, *Genealogical Research in Nova Scotia* (Halifax, Nova Scotia: Nimbus Publishing, Ltd., 1998), 10.
3. Angus Baxter, *In Search of Your British & Irish Roots: A Complete Guide to Tracing Your English, Welsh, Scottish & Irish Ancestors,* 4th ed. (Baltimore: Genealogical Publishing, 1999), 2.
4. The Internet Surname Database, www.surnamedb.com.
5. New England Historic Genealogical Society (NEHGS) research, or www.americanancestors.org; Maurice Whelan, burial 1837, St. Mary's Basilica, Halifax, Nova Scotia, No. 54, Family History Library #866363.
6. NEHGS research; Irish Family History Foundation, www.rootsireland.ie.
7. NEHGS research. Edward Whelan and Mary Wall marriage, 1832, St. Mary's Basilica, Halifax, Nova Scotia, marr. No. 37, Family History Library #866363.

CHAPTER 1: FAREWELL—AN ILL WIND BLOWS

1. Brian Fagan, *The Little Ice Age: How Climate Made History, 1300-1850* (New York: Basic Books/Perseus Books Group, 2000), 183.
2. Ibid, 185-186.

CHAPTER 2: MAURICE'S THOMASTOWN

1. Based on Maurice Whelan burial, 1837, St. Mary's Basilica, Halifax, Nova Scotia, No. 54, Family History Library #866363.
2. New England Historic Genealogical Society research, from Irish Family History Foundation, www.rootsireland.ie. Maurice Phelan and Eleanor Murphy, Church Marriage Record, 16 October 1796, Parish of Thomastown, County Kilkenny. Witnesses were Nicholas Ryan and Frances "Fanny" Orchard. (*For information about parishes, townlands and baronies, see related story,* Looking for Irish Ancestors: A Short Course.)
3. NEHGS researched the children of Maurice Phelan and Eleanor Murphy, locating information about them in Church Baptism Records

of County Kilkenny, as found on Irish Family History Foundation, www.rootsireland.ie. NEHGS noted that the five older children were baptized in Kilfane Chapel in Thomastown. The children: i. *Edward "Edmund" Phelan*, born or baptized 11 December 1796, Kilfane Chapel, Thomastown. Sponsors: Nicholas Ryan and Jony Connel. • ii. *Mary Phelan*, born or baptized 20 February 1798, Kilfane Chapel, Thomastown. Sponsors: Patrick Power and Judith Archer. • iii. *Elizabeth "Betty" Phelan*, born or baptized 20 June 1802, Kilfane Chapel, Thomastown. Sponsors: David Nolan and Catherine Spruhan. • iv. *Patrick "Patt" Phelan*, born or baptized 26 March 1807, Kilfane Chapel, Thomastown. Sponsors: Edward Nowlan and Jony Barry. • v. *Lawrence Phelan*, born or baptized 5 July 1809/1810 [See Chapter 4 Notes, #14.] • Sponsors: John Sheehy and Mary Butler. • vi. *Judith Phelan*, born or baptized 31 August 1811. Sponsors: John MacGrath and Catherine Power. • vii. *Michael Phelan*, born or baptized 22 May 1817. Sponsors: Thomas Deloughry and Ellen Cleary.

4. Determining the years Eleanor Murphy Phelan and Mary Murphy Phelan might have died was based on the baptism record of Michael Phelan, born or baptized 22 May 1817 in Thomastown, which lists Eleanor as his mother [Church Baptism Records of County Kilkenny, as found by NEHGS on Irish Family History Foundation, www.rootsireland.ie]; and on the baptism record of Ellen Phelan, born or baptized, 4 May 1821 in Thomastown, which lists her mother as Mary Murphy Phelan. Church Baptism Records of County Kilkenny, as found by NEHGS on Irish Family History Foundation, www.rootsireland.ie.

5. Based on Edward Whelan and Mary Wall marriage, 16 August 1832, St. Mary's Basilica, Halifax, Nova Scotia, marr. No. 37, Family History Library #866363.

6. Marilyn Silverman, *An Irish Working Class: Explorations in Political Economy and Hegemony, 1800-1950* (University of Toronto Press, 2001),4.

7. Ibid, 32.

8. Ibid., 4.

9. Thomastown Bridge, flooding: Ireland Department of Arts, Heritage and the Gaeltacht, ahg.gov.ie; www.irelandstats.com.

10. David Dickson, "Inland City: Reflections on Eighteenth Century Kilkenny," in *Kilkenny: History and Society*, 340.

11. Marilyn Silverman, *An Irish Working Class: Explorations in Political Economy and Hegemony, 1800-1950* (University of Toronto Press, 2001), 4-6.

12. Grennan Mill Craft School, www.kilkennyvec/ie/.../read/title/gren-

nan-mill-craft-school.

13. Silverman, *An Irish Working Class*, 6.

14. Ibid., 43.

15. Brian Fagan, *The Little Ice Age: How Climate Made History, 1300-1850* (New York: Basic Books/Perseus Books Group, 2000), 177-178.

16. Silverman, *An Irish Working Class*, 45.

17. Ibid, 44.

18. *The Oxford Companion to Irish History*, 438.

19. John Walsh, "The Hedge Schools," The Irish Cultural Society of Garden City, irish-society.org/home/hedgemaster-archives-2/groups-organizations/the-hedge-schools.

20. NEHGS research. Maurice Phelan and Eleanor Murphy, Church Marriage Record, 16 October 1796, Parish of Thomastown, County Kilkenny, as found on Irish Family History Foundation, www.rootsireland.ie.

21. Peter Higginbotham, "The Workhouse: The Story of an Institution," www.workhouses.org.uk/Thomastown.

22. Kerby A. Miller, *Emigrants and Exiles: Ireland and the Irish Exodus to North America* (Oxford University Press, 1985), 193-196.

23. *Encyclopaedia Britannica*, Online, www.britannica.com.

24. "The Great Famine of 1845," History Learning Site, 2006, historylearningsite.co.uk/ireland—greatfamine—of—1845.

CHAPTER 3: CONSIDERATIONS BEFORE EMIGRATING

1. Public Record Office of Northern Ireland (PRONI); www.proni.gov.uk.

2. Kerby A. Miller, *Emigrants and Exiles: Ireland and the Irish Exodus to North America* (Oxford University Press, 1985), 252.

3. PRONI

4. Samuel Lewis, *A Topographical Dictionary of Ireland*, 1837, Library Ireland; www.libraryireland.com/topog/t/thomastown-gowran-kilkenny.php.

5. Trail Kilkenny, River Walks, www.trailkilkenny.ie/activity-trails/river-walks.

CHAPTER 4: HALIFAX, NOVA SCOTIA

1. Terrence M. Punch, *Erin's Sons: Irish Arrivals in Atlantic Canada, 1761-1853,*

vol. I (Baltimore: Genealogical Publishing, 2008), 97.

2. *Encyclopaedia Britannica*, Online, www.britannica.com.

3. *Canada History*, canadahistory.com.

4. Parks Canada, www.pc.gc.ca/eng/lhn-nhs/halifax/index.

5. Parks Canada, www.pc.gc.ca/lhn-nhs/halifax/natcul2.aspx.

6. *The Canadian Encyclopedia*, www.thecanadianencyclopedia.ca/en/article/ micmac-mikmaq.

7. Nova Scotia Museum: The Family of Provincial Museums, museum. gov.ns.ca.

8. "The Deportation of the Acadians, 1755-1762," Canada in the Making, www.canadiana.ca/citm/specifique/deportation.

9. Black Cultural Centre for Nova Scotia, www.bccns.com.

10. Mark G. McGowan, "Irish Catholics," in *Encyclopedia of Canada's Peoples*, www.multiculturalcanada.ca/encyclopediaa-z/18/4.

11. *The Canadian Encyclopedia*, www.thecanadianencyclopedia.com.

12. Burial record of Maurice Phelan, 28 May 1837, St. Mary's Basilica, Halifax, Nova Scotia, No. 54, Family History Library #866363.

13. Edward "Edmund" Phelan, son of Maurice Phelan and Eleanor Murphy Phelan, was born or baptized 11 December 1796, Kilfane Parish, Park, Thomastown, County Kilkenny, Ireland. He married Mary Wall, widow of carpenter Thomas Wall, 16 August 1832, at St. Mary's Basilica, in Halifax, Halifax County, Nova Scotia, Canada [marriage No. 37], Family History Library #866363; and (under name Edward Whelan) from Halifax Church Records, St. Mary's Roman Catholic Church, microfilm 11506, marriages 1830-1843]. Witnesses were Michael Bulger, Martin Magher and Thomas Sheehan. Edward "Edmund" Phelan and Mary Wall Phelan had a daughter, Ellen, baptized 5 January 1834, at the age of five days, at St. Mary's Basilica, Halifax; Ellen Phelan baptism, 1834, St. Mary's Basilica, Halifax, Nova Scotia, 1830-1835, page 389, Family History Library #866357.

14. *Note: Lawrence Phelan, son of Maurice Phelan and Eleanor Murphy Phelan, was born possibly 5 July 1809 or 5 July 1810. The difference in the years is based on two sources: Halifax, Nova Scotia's Holy Cross Cemetery burial information [microfilm 12050, #974, plot #C55], which cited labourer [Law]Lawrence's age at death on 30 December 1847 as 37 (hence possibly born in 1810), and Thomastown parish church baptism records found by the New England Historic Genealogical Society (NEHGS) through Irish Family History Foundation, www.rootsireland.ie, which indicate he was born or baptized 5 July 1809. There were two baptism records noted by NEHGS, showing different spellings of his first name: 1. "Laurence Phelan, Church Baptism Record, 1809, Parish of Thomastown, Co. Kilkenny",*

as found on Irish Family History Foundation, www.rootsireland.ie. (Sponsors noted here were John Sheehy and Mary Butler.) 2. "Lawrence Phalen, b./bapt. 5 July 1809. Church Baptism Records of Co. Kilkenny", as found on Irish Family History Foundation, www. rootsireland.ie.

Lawrence Phelan married Ann Johnston, daughter of Loyd [sic] and Catherine (Golden) Johnston, 27 November 1833 in Halifax at St. Mary's Basilica. Witnesses were Michael Phelan and Honora Nolan. Another record, from St. Mary's Basilica, spells the bride's and groom's names differently, noting: "Lawrence Whelan and Ann Jonstan marriage, 1833, St. Mary's Basilica, Halifax, Nova Scotia, marr. No. 112," as found by NEHGS in Family History Library #866363. Ann Johnston was born circa May 1812 in County Mayo, Ireland, based on information in the above marriage record. Ann died of cancer 24 November 1885 in Essex County, Salem, Massachusetts; Massachusetts Vital Records, vol. 15, page 151, No. 567.

The couple had six children:

i. *Margaret Phelan,* baptized 3 April 1834, at age four days, St. Mary's Basilica, Halifax, Nova Scotia, 1830-1835, page 409. Sponsors: John Keys and Mary Lyons. Family History Library #866357; NEHGS. • ii. *Marianne Phelan,* baptized 15 March 1836, at age three days; St. Mary's Basilica, Halifax, Nova Scotia, 1835-1840, page 42. Sponsors: Michael Phelan and Mary Power. Family History Library #866357; NEHGS. • iii. *Lawrence Phelan,* baptized 12 May 1838, at the age of one week; St. Mary's Basilica, Halifax, Nova Scotia, 1835-1840, page 185. Sponsors: Michael Whelan and Ann Kelly. Family History Library #866357; NEHGS. • iv. *Edward Augustus Phelan,* baptized 20 July 1840 at the age of one day; St. Mary's Basilica, Halifax, Nova Scotia, 1835-1840, page 327. Sponsors: James [Macilue] and Margaret [Elwora]. Family History Library #866357; NEHGS. • v. *Michel [Michael] William Phelan,* baptized 4 September 1842, at the age of eight days; St. Mary's Basilica, Halifax, Nova Scotia, 1841-1844, page 160. Sponsors: Hugh MacNamara and Jane Nugent. [She likely was the sister-in-law of Michael's father.] Family History Library #866357; NEHGS. • vi. *Ellen Phelan,* baptized 13 April 1845, at the age of six days; St. Mary's Basilica, Halifax, Nova Scotia, No 88. Sponsors: John Walsh and Catherine Nugent. Family History Library #866357; NEHGS.

15. Michael Phelan, son of Maurice Phelan and Eleanor Murphy Phelan, was born or baptized 22 May 1817, in Thomastown Parish, County Kilkenny, Ireland. He married Jane Nugent, daughter of John Nugent and Anne Cantfield [or Caulford] Nugent of Halifax 20 February 1841 in

Halifax County, Nova Scotia, Canada, in the presence of Thomas Hogan, Marianne Nugent and Anne Cantfield [from St. Mary's Roman Catholic Church records, 1830-1843, microfilm 11506, and family research]. Jane was born about 1823 in Nova Scotia, Canada [from 1850 U.S. Census information, Michael Phaland household, Salem, Massachusetts, Essex County, p. 200, Dwelling No. 158, microfilm publication M432, roll 312: National Archives]. The couple had four children, a son and a daughter born in Halifax, and a daughter and a son born in Massachusetts. Michael, a tailor, according to the 1850 U.S. Census report, died after age 50 (the exact date and location of his death were not found.) Michael and Jane's children: i. *John Whelan (Phelan)*, born 25 June 1843, baptized St. Mary's Basilica, 26 June 1843, Halifax, Nova Scotia, 1841-1844, page 239, Family History Library #866357. Sponsors: Thomas Granville and Elizabeth Fitzgerald. • ii. *Elenor Whealon (Phelan)*, born 30 September, 1844, baptized 1 October 1844, Halifax, Nova Scotia, 1841-1844, page 7, Family History Library #866357. Sponsors: Patrick Coleman and Elizabeth Nugent. • iii. *Catherine Francis Phalen*, born about June 1848, baptized 18 September 1848, Salem, Massachusetts. Salem Vital Records to 1850, vol. 2, page 417, as found on www.americanancestors.org. • iv. *Michael Thomas Phalen*, born about September 1849, baptized 29 October 1849, Salem, Massachusetts. Salem Vital Records to 1850, vol. 2, page 161, as found on www.americanancestors.org.

16. Article by Peter Toner, 2008, in *The Canadian Encyclopedia*, www.canadianencyclopedia.ca/en/article/irish.

CHAPTER 5: A FUTURE IN AMERICA

1. Grand Trunk Railway article by James Marsh, 2006, in *The Canadian Encyclopedia*, www.thecanadianencyclopedia.com.

2. Phyllis R. Blakely, "Cunard, Sir Samuel," in *Dictionary of Canadian Biography*, vol. 9, (University of Toronto, 1976).

3. Massachusetts location from 1850 U.S. Census information, Michael Phaland household, Salem, Massachusetts, Essex County, page 200, Dwelling No. 158, microfilm publication M432, roll 312: National Archives.

4. Family research, 1850 U.S. Census.

5. Ann Phalen certificate of death, 24 November 1885, age seventy-three and six months, occupation, nurse. Commonwealth of Massachusetts, City of Salem death records, vol. 15, page 151, No. 567.

6. Marriage of Margaret Phalen to Benjamin Savory, 17 March 1853, Marble-

head, Mass., Massachusetts Vital Records, Marriages, 1853, vol. 69, page 243.

7. "Married," *Salem Register,* Salem, Mass., 28 March 1853, page 2.

8. *Acadian Recorder*, Halifax, Nova Scotia, Jean M. Holder, compiler, Vital Statistics from Halifax Newspapers, 1852-1854 (Halifax, Nova Scotia: Genealogical Association of the Royal Nova Scotia Historical Society, 1988), 86.

9. Ann Phalen did not appear in Salem, Mass., city directories until 1855, New England Historic Genealogical Society research (NEHGS). She and some family members were accounted for in the 1855 Mass. State census (family research).

10. Family research of the 1860 U.S. Census showed that Ann and members of her family were living in Salem, Mass.

11. Salem Directory, 1850; U.S. Census.

12. *Encyclopaedia Britannica*, Online, britannica.com.

13. Salem Directory, 1864.

14. Ellen Phalen (also known as Elinor or Eleanor in various records) married Charles H. Dalton, a currier, on April 28, 1863, from Massachusetts Vital Records, Marriages, 1863, vol. 162, page 202, and marriage announcement in the *Salem Register*, May 7, 1863, page 27.

CHAPTER 6: THE CIVIL WAR YEARS—1861-1865

1. *Africans in America*, "Judgment Day," part 4 of series, 1831-1865, Public Broadcasting Service, www.pbs.org/wgbh/aia/home.html.

2. "Poets, Shoemakers, and Freedom Seekers: Abolitionists and the Underground Railroad in Essex County," Salem Maritime National Historic Site, National Park Service, U.S. Department of the Interior, www.nps.gov/sama/historyculture.

3. Republican Party, www.gop.com.

4. Christian G. Samito. Introduction to the 2000 edition of *The History of the Ninth Regiment Massachusetts Volunteer Infantry, June 1861-June 1864,* by Daniel George Macnamara (New York: Fordham University Press, 2000), xv.

5. *The Civil War Society's Encyclopedia of the Civil War* (Wings Books, a division of Random House Value Publishing, 1997), 183. (Published by arrangement with The Philip Lief Group, Inc., Princeton, New Jersey.)

6. Ibid., 183.

Chapter 7: The Fighting Irish

1. Matthew Brennan, "The Irish Brigade: Heroes of the Civil War," in the digital edition of *Irish America*, irishamerica.com/... Irish brigade-heroes-of-the-civil-war, June/July 2011.

2. Christian G. Samito. Prologue to *Commanding Boston's Irish Ninth: The Civil War Letters of Colonel Patrick R. Guiney, Ninth Massachusetts Volunteer Infantry*, edited by Christian G. Samito (New York: Fordham University Press), xxiii.

3. Susannah Ural Bruce, *The Harp and the Eagle: Irish-American Volunteers and the Union Army, 1861-1865* (New York: New York University Press, 2006), 2.

4. The Civil War Trust, www.civilwar.org.

5. *Encyclopaedia Britannica*, Online, www.britannica.com.

6. Bruce, *The Harp and the Eagle*, 145.

7. *Encyclopaedia Britannica*, Online, www.britannica.com.

8. James M. McPherson, *Ordeal by Fire: The Civil War and Reconstruction*, 3rd ed. (New York: McGraw Hill, 2001), 384.

9. *Encyclopaedia Britannica*, Online, www.britannica.com.

10. McPherson, *Ordeal by Fire*, 385.

11. Ibid, 385.

12. Ibid, 384-385.

Chapter 8: Michael William Phalen

1. Daniel George Macnamara, *The History of the Ninth Regiment, Massachusetts Volunteer Infantry, June 1861-June 1864* (New York: Fordham University Press, 2000), 4-5; originally published by E.B. Stillings & Co. of Boston, Massachusetts, in 1899. This edition has an introduction by author Christian G. Samito.

2. American Civil War Research Database, www.civilwardata.com/ca_demo2.

3. Memorial to comrade Michael William Phalen from the Illinois Commandery of the Military Order of the Loyal Legion of the United States (MOLLUS). He was elected an Original Companion of the First Class of MOLLUS through the commandery of Illinois on February 14, 1895.

4. Macnamara, *The History of the Ninth Regiment*, 476.

5. Roster of the Ninth Regiment, *The History of the Ninth Regiment*, 486,

and 26; *Massachusetts Soldiers, Sailors, and Marines in the Civil War,* compiled and published by the Adjutant General, Norwood Press, 1931; U.S. National Archives and Records Administration (NARA), U.S. Army medical/pension records.

6. NARA, U.S. Army medical/pension records.

7. Illinois MOLLUS memorial to Michael William Phalen.

8. Ibid.

9. Massachusetts Civil War Research Center, www.massachusettscivil-war.com; Macnamara, *The History of the Ninth Regiment,* 2-9.

10. Boston Tea Party Ships & Museum, www.bostonteapartyship.com.

11. Macnamara, *The History of the Ninth Regiment,* 7.

12. Ibid, 8.

13. Ibid., 6.

14. Frank Flynn. "'The Fighting Ninth'for Fifty Years and the Semicentennial Celebration," a regimental anniversary celebration with remarks from Flynn based on Daniel George Macnamara's *The History of the Ninth Regiment.*

15. Edward Rowe Snow, *The Islands of Boston Harbor* (Beverly, Mass: Commonwealth Editions, 2002), 180-182. Originally published in 1935, the book was updated by Jeremy D'Entremont and has a foreward by William M. Fowler, Jr.

16. Macnamara, *The History of the Ninth Regiment,* 10.

17. Ibid., 10-12.

18. Ibid., 13-14.

19. Ibid., 22.

20. Ibid., 22-24; and Christian G. Samito, book Introduction, xviii.

21. Flynn, "'The Fighting Ninth for Fifty Years.'"

22. Christian G. Samito, *Becoming American Under Fire: Irish Americans, African Americans, and the Politics of Citizenship During the Civil War Era* (Ithaca, New York: Cornell University Press, 2009), 106.

23. Macnamara, *The History of the Ninth Regiment,* 166-168.

24. Ibid., Roster of the Ninth Regiment, 429.

CHAPTER 9: INTO THE BATTLE

1. Daniel George Macnamara, *The History of the Ninth Regiment, Massachusetts Volunteer Infantry, June 1861-June 1864* (New York: Fordham University Press, 2000), 28-30; originally published by E.B. Stillings & Co. of Bos-

ton, Massachusetts, in 1899. This edition has an introduction by author Christian G. Samito; and Samito, ed., *Commanding Boston's Irish Ninth: The Civil War Letters of Colonel Patrick R. Guiney, Ninth Massachusetts Volunteer Infantry,* (New York: Fordham University Press, 1998), 10.

2. Timothy J. Regan, *The Lost Civil War Diaries: The Diaries of of Corporal Timothy J. Regan,* eds. David C.Newton and Kenneth J. Pluskat (Victoria, B.C., Canada: Trafford Publishing, 2003), 24.

3. Ibid., 31.

4. Susannah Ural Bruce, *The Harp and the Eagle: Irish-American Volunteers and the Union Army, 1861-1865* (New York: New York University Press, 2006), 96-98.

5. Edward Longacre, "Army of the Potomac," in *Encyclopedia Virginia.* Virginia Foundation for the Humanities, April 19, 2012, www.encyclopedia-virginia.org/army_of_the_potomac.

6. James M. McPherson, *Ordeal by Fire: The Civil War and Reconstruction,* 3rd ed. (New York: McGraw Hill, 2001), 215.

7. Macnamara, *The History of the Ninth Regiment,* 43.

8. Ibid., Preface, viii.

9. Ibid., 43.

10. Battle dates compiled from: Massachusetts Civil War Research Center, www.massachusettscivilwar.com; "Civil War in the East: A Reference Guide to America's War in the East," http://civilwarintheeast.com/usa/ma/ma09.php; U.S. National Park Service, www.nps.gov; *(See related section,* Addendum: A Memorial for a Civil War Veteran *for additional battles in which the Ninth participated.)*

11. William F. Fox, *Regimental Losses in the American Civil War, 1861-1865,* (Albany Publishing, 1889) 157.

12. Macnamara, *The History of the Ninth Regiment,* 162.

13. *Encyclopedia Virginia,* www.encyclopediavirginia.org/gaines_s_mill_battle.

14. Macnamara, *The History of the Ninth Regiment,* 158.

15. Massachusetts Civil War Research Center; from documents of the Adjutant General's Office of Massachusetts, 1888.

16. Macnamara, *The History of the Ninth Regiment,* 162.

17. *Encyclopedia Virginia,* www.encyclopediavirginia.org/malvern_hill_battle.

18. Macnamara, *The History of the Ninth Regiment,* 159.

19. Memorial to comrade Michael William Phalen from the Illinois

Commandery of the Military Order of the Loyal Legion of the United States (MOLLUS).

20. *Commanding Boston's Irish Ninth: The Civil War Letters of Colonel Patrick R. Guiney, Ninth Massachusetts Volunteer Infantry*, ed. Christian G. Samito (New York: Fordham University Press, 1998); from "Prologue: The Drums of War," xi, xiii, xiv.

21. Samito, ed., *Commanding Boston's Irish Ninth*, Preface, ix.

22. Samito, ed., *Commanding Boston's Irish Ninth*, Prologue, xxvii-xxviii.

23. Macnamara, *The History of the Ninth Regiment*, 155.

24. Ibid., 158-159.

25. *Commanding Boston's Irish Ninth*, 127.

26. Ibid., 120.

27. Ibid., 125-126. Additionally, Samito, in a footnote page 126, writes that the original communication from Father Scully to Governor John A. Andrew is located in the Ninth Massachusetts File in the Executive Department Letters, Massachusetts State Archives, Boston Massachusetts.

28. Ibid., 126.

29. Ibid., footnote 139.

CHAPTER 10: PROVING HIS METTLE

1. Daniel George Macnamara, *The History of the Ninth Regiment, Massachusetts Volunteer Infantry, June 1861-June 1864* (New York: Fordham University Press, 2000), 31; originally published by E.B. Stillings & Co. of Boston, Massachusetts, in 1899. This edition has an introduction by author Christian G. Samito.

2. Ibid., 356.

3. U.S. National Archives and Records Administration (NARA), U.S. Army records.

4. Ibid.

5. Ibid.

6. *Commanding Boston's Irish Ninth: The Civil War Letters of Colonel Patrick R. Guiney, Ninth Massachusetts Volunteer Infantry*, ed. Christian G. Samito (New York: Fordham University Press, 1998), 189.

7. Macnamara, *The History of the Ninth Regiment*, 304.

8. *Commanding Boston's Irish Ninth*, 193.

9. Died, *Salem Register*, May 18, 1863, page 2.

10. Massachusetts Vital Records, Deaths; and Deaths Registered in the

City of Boston, where Ellen J. Fay Phalen, formerly of Ireland, is noted as age 21, married, and the daughter of Edward and Mary Fay of Ireland; both state and city records are found in year 1863, vol. 167, page 60.

11. NARA, U.S. Army records.

12. "War Items and Incidents," *Salem Register*, May 21, 1863, page 2.

13. *Commanding Boston's Irish Ninth*, 199.

14. Ibid., 208.

15. NARA, U.S. Army medical records.

16. Ibid.

17. Macnamara, *The History of the Ninth Regiment*, 351.

18. *Commanding Boston's Irish Ninth*, 242.

19. Samito, ed., *Commanding Boston's Irish Ninth*, 240.

20. Timothy J. Regan, *The Lost Civil War Diaries: The Diaries of of Corporal Timothy J. Regan,* eds. David C.Newton and Kenneth J. Pluskat (Victoria, B.C., Canada: Trafford Publishing, 2003), 124.

21. Macnamara, *The History of the Ninth Regiment*, 278.

22. Ibid., 278-279.

23. Regan, *The Lost Civil War Diaries*, 128.

24. *Commanding Boston's Irish Ninth*, 215-216.

25. Samito, ed., *Commanding Boston's Irish Ninth*, 245 and 249.

26. Macnamara, *The History of the Ninth Regiment*, 407.

27. Ibid., 393.

28. Ibid., 412-419.

CHAPTER II: A HOMECOMING—STARTING OVER

1. Salem Directory, 1864.

2. Massachusetts Marriages, 1841-1915. Michael W. Phalen, 22, son of Lawrence and Anna [sic] Phalen, married Margaret Ryan, daughter of Patrick and Honora Ryan, August 22, 1864, in Salem, Massachusetts; obtained through familysearch.org, the Church of Jesus Christ of Latter-Day Saints; record number 190; film number 1433021; digital folder number 4332357; image number 00670; www.ancestry.com cites the same Massachusetts marriage record, citing the wife as Margaret Ryun [sic], born about 1844.

3. Filling in the blanks in a Declaration for Pension form in February of 1907, Michael W. Phalen declared that after leaving the service he had lived in two places in 1864, Salem, Mass., and then Chicago. Family re-

search placed him in Chicago at least since 1866.

4. Susannah Ural Bruce, *The Harp and the Eagle: Irish-American Volunteers and the Union Army, 1861-1865* (New York: New York University Press, 2006), 147.

5. Family research.

6. Christian G. Samito, *Becoming American Under Fire: Irish Americans, African Americans, and the Politics of Citizenship During the Civil War Era* (Ithaca, New York: Cornell University Press, 2009), 2.

7. Military Order of the Loyal Legion of the United States (MOLLUS), suvcw.org/mollus.htm.

8. Noted in memorial to comrade Michael William Phalen from the Illinois Commandery of the Military Order of the Loyal Legion of the United States (MOLLUS).

9. Internet Archive, the Library of Congress, archive.org/details/historyofgeorgeh00cook; an address by Henry C. Cooke on the post's 25th anniversary; published in 1898 by F. Kressman & Bros., Chicago.

10. From memorial to Michael William Phalen, Illinois Commandery, MOLLUS.

Chapter 12: A New Horizon—Chicago

1. U.S. National Archives and Records Administration (NARA), U.S. Army pension records. In a 1907 notarized pension request, Michael W. Phalen said he had lived in Salem, Massachusetts, in 1864, and then Chicago, Illinois, in 1864 as well; and family lore.

2. Michael F. Funchion, "The Irish of Chicago," Northern Illinois University Libraries, www.lib.niu.edu/1999/iht629912.

3. *Encyclopedia of Chicago*, www.encyclopedia.chicagohistory.org.

4. Family lore.

5. Family lore and Calvary Catholic Cemetery burial record.

6. Infant Mortality, *Encyclopedia of Children and Childhood in History and Society*, www.faqs.org/childhood.

7. Calvary Catholic Cemetery record.

8. Family research.

9. Family lore.

10. Donald L. Miller, *City of the Century: The Epic of Chicago and the Making of America* (New York: Simon & Schuster), 1996), 151.

11. William Cronon, *Nature's Metropolis: Chicago and the Great West* (New York: W.W. Norton & Co., 1991), 345.

12. Donald L. Miller, *City of the Century*, 159.

13. Family lore and noted in memorial to comrade Michael William Phalen from the Illinois Commandery of the Military Order of the Loyal Legion of the United States (MOLLUS).

14. Ibid.

15. Family lore and research.

16. William Cronon, *Nature's Metropolis*, 345.

17. Death of Maggie C. Phalen, born in Ireland, due to consumption, at age 30 years, on March 3, 1873. Department of Health of the City of Chicago, Bureau of Vital Statistics, Cook County, Illinois; death certificate record, page 165, line 36. Duration of disease, four months. Burial at Calvary Catholic Cemetery, Evanston, Illinois.

18. Margaret Phalen was interred at Calvary Catholic Cemetery in Evanston, Illinois, on April 16, 1873; cemetery burial record.

Chapter 13: Moving On With Life

1. U.S. National Archives and Records Administration (NARA), U.S. Army widow's pension records. Testimony of relatives of Mary H. Curtin during pension request proceedings.

2. Records of Phalen burials at Calvary Catholic Cemetery, Evanston, Illinois.

3. Information about the Travelers Protective Association comes from the memorial to Michael William Phalen from the Illinois Commandery of the Military Order of the Loyal Legion of the United States (MOLLUS), and from website www.tpahq.org/detailed history. Information about Atha & Illingworth comes from The Navy Department Library, www.history.navy.mil/library//special/contract.

Chapter 14: A New 'War'—A Bureaucratic Skirmish

1. Michael William Phalen's medical/pension request proceedings, Department of the Interior Bureau of Pensions, 1892-1907; U.S. National Archives and Records Administration (NARA).

2. Pension Act of 1890, Statutes at Large, 51st Congress, pages 182-183.

3.-11. NARA, Michael William Phalen's medical/pension records, the Department of the Interior Bureau of Pensions, 1892-1907.

12. Death certificate for Michael William Phalen, Department of Health

of the City of Chicago, Bureau of Vital Statistics, Cook County, Illinois.

13. Michel [Michael] William, baptized 4 September 4, 1842, at the age of eight days; St. Mary's Basilica, Halifax, Nova Scotia, 1841-1844, page 160. Family History Library #866357.

14. NARA, Michael William Phalen's medical/pension request proceedings.

15. Ibid.

16. *Encyclopaedia Britannica*, Online, www.britannica.com.

17. Ripon Historical Society, "A History of the Oil Lamp in America," www.riponhistory.com/museum-and-archives/american-oil.

18. *Encyclopedia of Chicago*, www.encyclopedia.chicagohistory.org.

CHAPTER 15: EDWARD AUGUSTUS PHALEN

1. *Massachusetts Soldiers, Sailors, and Marines in the Civil War*, compiled and published by the Adjutant General, Norwood Press, 1931; promotion from second lieutenant to first lieutenant noted in *Salem Register* under "War Items and Incidents," December 1, 1862, page 2.

2. U.S. National Archives and Records Administration (NARA) records.

3. *Massachusetts Soldiers, Sailors, and Marines in the Civil War.*

4. *A Legacy of Valor: The Memoirs and Letters of Captain Henry Newton Comey, 2nd Massachusetts Infantry,* ed. Lyman Richard Comey, part of the *Voices of the Civil War Series,* ed. Peter S. Carmichael (Knoxville: The University of Tennessee Press, 2004), 11-12. (Henry Newton Comey was Lyman Richard Comey's great-grandfather's cousin.)

CHAPTER 16: INTO THE FRAY

1. *The Civil War Society's Encyclopedia of the Civil War* (Wings Books, a division of Random House Value Publishing, 1997), 20-22 and 327. (Published by arrangement with The Philip Lief Group, Inc., Princeton, New Jersey.)

2. *Massachusetts Soldiers, Sailors, and Marines in the Civil War*, compiled and published by the Adjutant General, Norwood Press, 1931; National Park Service, www.nps.gov/history/hps/abpp/battles; through U.S. National Archives and Records Administration (NARA), U.S. Army medical/pension records.

3. Civil War Trust, www.civilwar.org/battlefields/cedar mountain.

4. *A Legacy of Valor: The Memoirs and Letters of Captain Henry Newton Comey, 2nd Massachusetts Infantry,* ed. Lyman Richard Comey, part of the *Voices of the Civil War Series,* ed. Peter S. Carmichael (Knoxville: The University of Tennessee Press, 2004), 59.

5. The Battle of Cedar Mountain, Official Report of Gen. Pope, Headquarters Army of Virginia, Cedar Mountain. Aug. 13, 1862; NARA records.

6. *A Legacy of Valor,* 64.

7. *A Legacy of Valor,* 66. How Edward Augustus Phalen got to the hospital is surmised from a letter that Henry Newton Comey had sent to his father; in it he described how a sergeant who was shot in the back "was removed by our ambulance wagon and sent on to a hospital in Alexandria ..."

8. NARA, U.S. Army records.

9. Civil War Washington, Field Records of Hospitals, 1821-1912, Manuscript Record Group 94, National Archives, obtained through the Center for Digital Research in the Digital Humanities, University of Nebraska-Lincoln, civilwardc.org/data/places/view/500.

10. "Battle of Cedar Mountain," *Salem Register*, page 3.

11. NARA, U.S. Army medical/pension records.

12. *New York Times* story, August 13,1862, www.nytimes.com/1862/08/13/news/the-sick-and-wounded-on-davids-island.

13. NARA, U.S. Army medical/pension records.

14. NARA, U.S. Army records.

15. *A Legacy of Valor,* 201 and 202.

16. Ibid., 237. In his memoir, Henry Newton Comey wrote: "On April 9th Captains Mehan and Phalen returned to the regiment. Because we were extremely short on enlisted men and over strength with officers," he noted, he, along with others, were sent "back to Massachusetts to recruit more men for the regiment."

17. Ibid.

18. Regimental report, NARA Army records.

19. *Massachusetts Soldiers, Sailors, and Marines in the Civil War.*

20. Family research; William C. Phalen, born 1877, ancestry.com.

21. NARA, U.S. Army medical/pension records.

22.-24., Ibid.

CHAPTER 17: A CALL FOR HELP

1. U.S. National Archives and Records Administration (NARA); medical/pension records.

2. 54th Congress, "Memorial Addresses on the Life and Character of William Cogswell, late a Representative from Massachusetts," delivered in the House of Representatives and Senate; from Biographical Directory of the United States, www.bioguide.congress.gov.

3. NARA, U.S. Army medical/pension records.

4.-18., Ibid.

19. Office of City Clerk, Salem, Commonwealth of Massachusetts; Massachusetts Vital Records, vol. 18, page 95, No.198.

20. NARA, U.S. Army medical/pension records.

21. "Recent Deaths," *Boston Journal,* Boston, Massachusetts, April 16, 1894, page 6.

EPILOGUE: SOME REFLECTIONS FROM BILL PHALEN

1. Terrence M. Punch, *Erin's Sons: Irish Arrivals in Atlantic Canada, 1761-1853,* vol. I (Baltimore: Genealogical Publishing, 2008), 13 and 34.

2. Salem City Directory, 1916, page 384.

3. Records of widows' pension dealings with the Department of Interior Bureau of Pensions for the wives of former Union Army officers Michael W. Phalen and Edward A. Phalen were obtained from the U.S. National Archives and Records Administration (NARA). Records include testimony of relatives and others.

4. Margaret Phalen Savory was living in Salem, Mass., at the time of her death on May 8, 1909, from Massachusetts Vital Records, Deaths, 1909, vol. 84, page 133. Sister Ellen Phalen Dalton was living in Boston at the time of brother Michael W. Phalen's death in 1908, from NARA records.

LOOKING FOR IRISH ANCESTORS: A SHORT COURSE

1. Marilyn Silverman and P.H. Gulliver, "Social Life and Local Meaning: The Case of Contemporary Thomastown," in *Kilkenny: History and Society,* eds. William Nolan and Kevin Whelan (Dublin: Geography Publications, 1990), 594.

2. Church Marriage Record, 1796, Thomastown parish, County Kilken-

ny, www.roootsireland.ie; baptism of Michael Phelan in 1817, lists his mother as Eleanor Murphy; NEHGS research.

3. Angus Baxter, *In Search of Your British & Irish Roots: A Complete Guide to Tracing Your English, Welsh, Scottish, & Irish Ancestors*, 4th ed. (Baltimore: Genealogical Publishing), 243.

4. *The Oxford Companion to Irish History*, ed. S.J. Connolly, (Oxford University Press, 1998), 547.

5. Deirdre Flanagan and Laurence Flanagan, *Irish Place Names* (Gill & MacMillan, 1994), 1.

6. Baxter, *In Search of Your British & Irish Roots*, 243.

7. *The Oxford Companion to Irish History*, 39.

8. Baxter, *In Search of Your British & Irish Roots*, 243.

9. *The Oxford Companion to Irish History*, 444.

10. Marilyn Silverman, *An Irish Working Class: Explorations in Political Economy and Hegemony, 1800-1950* (Toronto: University of Toronto Press, 2001), 4.

Electronic/Internet sources were obtained between March 2013 and August 2014.

BIBLIOGRAPHY

Baxter, Angus. *In Search of Your British & Irish Roots: A Complete Guide to Tracing Your English, Welsh, Scottish, and Irish Ancestors.* Baltimore: Genealogical Publishing Co., 1991.

Bruce, Susannah Ural. *The Harp and the Eagle: Irish-American Volunteers and the Union Army, 1861-1865.* New York: New York University Press, 2006.

Comey, Henry Newton. *A Legacy of Valor: The Memoirs and Letters of Captain Henry Newton Comey, 2nd Massachusetts Infantry.* Lyman Richard Comey, ed. Knoxville, Tenn.: The University of Tennessee Press, 2004.

Connolly, S.J., ed. *The Oxford Companion to Irish History.* Oxford: Oxford University Press, 1998.

Cronon, William. *Nature's Metropolis: Chicago and the Great West.* New York: W.W. Norton & Company, Inc., 1991.

Fagan, Brian. *The Little Ice Age: How Climate Made History, 1300-1850.* New York: Basic Books, a Member of the Perseus Books Groups, 2002.

Flanagan, Deirdre, and Laurence Flanagan. *Irish Place Names.* Dublin: Gill & Macmillan, Ltd., 2002.

Flynn, Frank J. *The Fighting Ninth for Fifty Years and the Semi-Centennial Celebration.* Emory University Digital Library Publications Program, electronic source, transcript of 1911 manuscript.

Gulliver, P.H., and Marilyn Silverman, "Social Life and Local Meaning: The Case of Contemporary Thomastown," in *Kilkenny: History and Society,* William Nolan and Kevin Whelan, eds. Dublin: Geography Publications, 1990.

LeVert, Suzanne, principal writer and researcher. *The Civil War Society's Encyclopedia of the Civil War.* Stephen Francoeur and Gary M. Sunshine, eds. New York: Wings Books, a division of Random House Value Publishing, Inc., by arrangement with The Philip Lief Group, Inc., 1997

Macnamara, Daniel G. *The History of the Ninth Regiment Massachusetts Volunteer Infantry, June, 1861-June, 1864*. Introduction by Christian G. Samito. Boston: E.B. Stillings & Co., 1899. Reprint, New York: Fordham University Press, 2000.

McPherson, James M. *Ordeal by Fire: The Civil War and Reconstruction*, Third Edition. New York: McGraw-Hill Higher Education, a Division of the McGraw-Hill Companies, 2001.

Miller, Donald L. *City of the Century: The Epic of Chicago and the Making of America*. New York: Simon & Schuster., 1996.

Miller, Kerby A. *Emigrants and Exiles: Ireland and the Irish Exodus to North America*. Oxford: Oxford University Press, 1985.

Punch, Terrence M. *Erin's Sons: Irish Arrivals in Atlantic Canada, 1761-1853*, Volumes I and II. Baltimore: Genealogical Publishing Co., 2008.

Punch, Terrence M. *Genealogical Research in Nova Scotia*. Halifax, Nova Scotia: Nimbus Publishing Limited, 1998.

Regan, Timothy J. *The Lost Civil War Diaries: The Diaries of Corporal Timothy J. Regan*. David C. Newton, and Kenneth J. Pluskat, eds. From the private collection of Kenneth J. Pluskat. Victoria, B.C., Canada: Trafford Publishing, 2003.

Samito, Christian G. *Becoming American Under Fire: Irish Americans, African Americans, and the Politics of Citizenship During the Civil War Era*. Ithaca, New York: Cornell University Press, 2009.

Samito, Christian G., ed. *Commanding Boston's Irish Ninth: The Civil War Letters of Colonel Patrick R. Guiney, Ninth Massachusetts Volunteer Infantry*. New York: Fordham University Press, 1998.

Silverman, Marilyn. *An Irish Working Class: Explorations in Political Economy and Hegemony, 1800-1950*. Toronto: University of Toronto Press, Inc., 2001.

Snow, Edward Rowe. *The Islands of Boston Harbor.* Reprint of 1935 edition, updated by Jeremy D'Entremont, with foreward by William M.Fowler, Jr. Beverly, Mass.: Commonwealth Editions, an imprint of Memoirs Unlimited, Inc., 2002.